The Best War Ever

THE AMERICAN MOMENT

Stanley I. Kutler

Series Editor

The Best War Ever

America and World War II

Second Edition

MICHAEL C. C. ADAMS

Johns Hopkins University Press

Baltimore

© 1994, 2015 Johns Hopkins University Press
All rights reserved. Published 2015
Printed in the United States of America on acid-free paper

2 4 6 8 9 7 5 3 1

The Johns Hopkins University Press
2715 North Charles Street
Baltimore, Maryland 21218-4363
www.press.jhu.edu

Library of Congress Cataloging-in-Publication Data
Adams, Michael C. C., 1945–
The best war ever : America and World War II / Michael C. C. Adams. —
Second edition.
pages cm. — (The American moment)
Includes bibliographical references and index.
ISBN 978-1-4214-1667-0 (pbk. : alk. paper) — ISBN 978-1-4214-1668-7 (electronic) —
ISBN 1-4214-1667-0 (pbk. : alk. paper) — ISBN 1-4214-1668-9 (electronic)
1. World War, 1939–1945—United States. 2. United States—History—1933–1945.
I. Title.
D769.A56 2015
940.540973—dc23   2014029354

A catalog record for this book is available from the British Library.

Special discounts are available for bulk purchases of this book.
For more information, please contact Special Sales at 410-516-6936 or
specialsales@press.jhu.edu.

Johns Hopkins University Press uses environmentally friendly book materials,
including recycled text paper that is composed of at least 30 percent
post-consumer waste, whenever possible.

To
David A. Steves
Geoffrey R. Glier
Christopher T. Adams

Brothers of Mine

CONTENTS

ILLUSTRATIONS

MAPS

The Best War Ever was first published in 1994, with the stated purpose of presenting a balanced view of World War II that avoided the extremes of glorification ("This was the Good War") and vilification ("We were no better than our enemies"). The concept seems to have succeeded, as the book has found favor with many readers, especially undergraduates and their professors. It has gone through nine printings.

Having reached the twentieth anniversary of publication, a good lifetime for any book of its kind, a decision had to be made as to whether we would produce a second edition or should let the work sink into a quiet scholarly grave. For many years, I was not convinced that revisions would add much to our picture of the war. Recently, however, I have concluded that developments in historical understanding and changing contemporary interests justify a new edition. For example, the debate over the effectiveness and morality of the Western Allies' strategic bombing campaigns has moved forward.

As another instance, advances in medical science enable us to see that the personality damage sustained by combat veterans was rooted not only in reliving the nightmare emotionally (post-traumatic stress disorder) but also in radical physical wounds to the head (traumatic brain injuries). The Walter Reed Army Medical Center now considers these conditions together. Due in part to the determined research of my fellow Northern Kentucky University Regents Professor, J. Robert Lilly, breaking a veil of silence, we now know significantly more about the widespread incidence of sexual assault by U.S. military personnel upon civilians, at least in the European theater.

On the home front, I underplayed in my original conception of the book the impact of the war on the nascent development of an American social welfare system, including Social Security and Medicare, perhaps because those issues were not such burning topics in 1994. These and other areas of current public interest that have roots in the war era are now woven into the text.

* * *

In a chapter on mythmaking and World War II, the first edition dealt with the rise of the Good War myth, along with the counterarguments of critics who challenged the triumphalist narrative. Although by 1994 it was clear how the dominant perception of the war was trending, veneration of the 1940s generation had not yet reached its peak. This came with the later work of revered historian Stephen E. Ambrose, along with the complementary writing of journalist Tom Brokaw, author of the phrase "the Greatest Generation" to describe 1940s Americans, and the further contributions of those who shared their views. We have now advanced sufficiently on the historical timeline to plot more fully the ascendency of the Good War legend.

By the late 1990s, it seemed that the popular presentation of the conflict as the "Best War Ever" had become fixed in the public mind as the legitimate version of the past and that this perception would not change. Yet, almost immediately in the twenty-first century, the centrality of the myth to American thought and action appeared to waiver, and the narrative seemingly has moved into eclipse. In a new chapter, called "The Life Cycle of a Myth" and placed appropriately at the end of the book, I chart the long struggle to define the nature of the war, the reasons that the romanticized version triumphed, and why this characterization suddenly seems less relevant in shaping attitudes and policies. I also try to delineate the societal pitfalls that occur when a flawed view of an earlier era is used to predicate present policies and public actions. History is never just a thing of the past, but an active factor in our lives: how deftly we interpret what has gone before helps to determine how well we perform today.

Suggestions for further reading can be found on the book's website at www.press.jhu.edu.

In presenting a second edition of *The Best War Ever*, I have just a few people to thank, but they are important. First, I am deeply grateful to the many students, teachers, and general readers who have made the book a success. NKU professor Bonnie May consistently used the book to draw her students into the enthralling study of history, and their penetrating questions when we talked showed repeatedly that they had engaged with their reading. Other NKU colleagues whose thoughts on war have helped the development of my own thinking include Nancy Kersell, Francois LeRoy, Burke Miller, James A. Ramage, Jonathan Reynolds, and W. Michael Ryan.

For many years, I guided a military history lecture series that allowed me to meet many gifted and prominent students of war. Several spring to mind for their provocative thinking on World War II: Professor D'Ann Campbell of Austin Peay State University; Larry Gara, emeritus professor at Wilmington College; Professor Michael D. Pearlman of the U.S. Army Command and General Staff College; and the late Professor Russell F. Weigley of Temple University.

Becky Clark of Johns Hopkins University Press played a crucial role in urging that we undertake a second edition, overcoming my initial skepticism. Robert J. Brugger, my editor, consistently supports viewing war realistically, and he has great patience with the quirks of authors. Juliana McCarthy, Managing Editor, and Andre Barnett, Senior Production Editor, are great facilitators. Glenn Perkins did a superb job of copyediting.

It is no mere conventional tip of the hat for me to express deep gratitude to my wife and colleague Susan Adams (formerly Kissel). As a feminist scholar, she taught me many years ago to see the whole of humanity, and not only adult white males, when considering war. Susan threw the considerable weight of her opinion behind the case for a second edition of *The Best War*, reminding me in particular how I have continued to track images of World War II in popular culture. And, of course, as an English professor, she perennially improves my use of the language.

For generations of Americans, World War II has been the historical reference point that transformed and defined the future path of their country. It is generally agreed that this was a necessary war. International aggression in Europe and Asia, carried out by nations claiming to be have-nots and trying to get what they thought they needed through conquest, brought untold misery to their victims and instability to the entire world. In Europe, Nazi aggression came to include a deliberate policy of genocide against those declared unfit to live under the Third Reich; in Asia, millions were murdered or brutalized by their Japanese conquerors. This rule by force, based on theories of ethnic superiority, had to be stopped. Western Allied victories in the European and Asian theaters demonstrated that systems based on parliamentary democracy and free enterprise could win a struggle with authoritarianism and militarism, then deemed more efficient in organizing society for the pursuit of national goals. This should always be recognized as a profound gain for the future of humankind.

Americans were justifiably proud of their immense contribution to the positive outcome. The United States had suffered deeply in the Great Depression of the 1930s, and some people even began to despair of the ability of capitalism and democracy to solve overriding economic problems. But then, from 1941 to 1945, the United States fought around the globe, throwing its enormous military and economic might behind Allied victory, and far from being depleted by this effort, emerged at war's end as the leader of the free world and the richest nation in human history. America shared this wealth generously with friend and former enemy alike, significantly aiding their recovery.

Over time, this very real achievement became mythologized into the best war we ever had. As America's economic predominance came to be challenged in the last decades of the twentieth century, and as problems at home and abroad became less tractable, Americans looking back came to see the war years as a golden age, an idyllic period when everything was simpler and a can-do generation of Americans solved the world's problems. In this mythic time of the Good War, everyone was supposed to have been united; there were no racial or gender tensions, no class conflicts. Things worked better then, we have been told, from kitchen gadgets to public schools. Families were well adjusted; kids read a lot and respected their elders; parents did not divorce. As with all myths, there is much truth in this popular picture, but it also involves significant distortion and simplification.

The reality of combat in World War II has been mythologized. Although we know that many veterans of later conflicts, from Vietnam to Iraq and Afghanistan, suffered post-traumatic stress disorder, it is commonly believed that nearly all World War II veterans adjusted quickly and easily. After all, they fought in a good war. Vietnam veterans, by contrast, took part in a "lesser" war, in which American troops, caught in an ugly situation, committed acts that later disturbed them and the public. In fact, as we shall see, the experience of combat in World War II was quite horrible and left lasting physical and mental scars on many combatants. Other stereotypes continued to prevail, such as that German officers were typically heel-clicking martinets and American generals were all rough and ready democratic improvisers.

The goal of this book is to subject the major aspects of the war to careful analysis in the hope of presenting a more realistic picture, one that does not demean the achievement of the United States and of liberal democracy but that at the same time does not diminish the stress, suffering, problems, and failures inevitably faced by a society at war. The nature of the task has dictated the scope of the work. This is more than a chronological narrative, and some aspects of the war experience, those most subject to myth-making, get more exposure than others. In addition, I discuss at length some facets of life in the period that usually receive little coverage. One example is the development of a teen culture, with its pervasive anti-intellectualism and pursuit of pleasure, sometimes ending in delinquency, a phenomenon of American society that critics usually assume appeared at a much later date. Also, today it is important to include detailed treatment of homosexuals in chapters on the armed forces and the civilian milieu during the war.

This book does not claim to be a definitive study of the war. I doubt that any work could claim that distinction, because our knowledge constantly changes, as does our sense of what is relevant or appropriate to study. What I hope to do is provoke in readers fresh thoughts and new questions about the experience of World War II, about the nature of war in general, and about this particular period in history. Overall, the book emphasizes throughout that history, unlike legend, is complex and cannot be boiled down to a fable of good versus bad.

In the seven chapters that follow, we examine, in a logical progression, major facets of the World War II experience. We begin by looking at the challenges facing statesmen between the two world wars, 1918 to 1939, and suggest that finding solutions to international problems was not as easy as some later polemicists have claimed. With the failure of diplomacy, the conflict came. We trace its dominant patterns and multifaceted character, being careful to note the contributions of all Allied participants to ultimate victory.

When the United States joins the conflict, it is important to profile the American war machine, noting its fundamental characteristics, its strengths and weaknesses. And we want to know, as millions of military personnel shipped overseas, what happened to the minority who engaged in combat. But, also, we should ask how Americans in general interacted with the many foreign noncombatants they encountered in both friendly and enemy countries.

For those who stayed at home, the war years brought great change, encouraging certain trends in American life while curtailing others. Several public sector choices made then, along with major shifts and developments in American life, derived from massive social and economic reorganization for war production in the private sector, molded the postwar American world far into the future. This was the changed country that soldiers came home to; we shall look at how well they adapted.

Finally, in the last chapter, after trying to envision a realistic picture of the war's history, I attempt to measure this actuality against the mythologized version of the era. I try to determine how and why a complex period of history became simplified into the popular story of the Best War Ever and examine some reasons why the widely accepted version of this Good War is now fading or being put aside, at least for the present, as seemingly less relevant to the situation facing us in the second decade of the twenty-first century.

The Best War Ever

CHAPTER ONE

No Easy Answers

A popular folklore version of World War II suggests that the war came for reasons that were straightforward and evident at the time. Between the wars, so the story goes, a group of dictators collaborated openly to destroy democracy and capitalism. These tyrants were Benito Mussolini in Italy, Francisco Franco in Spain, Adolf Hitler in Germany, and Emperor Hirohito in Japan. They committed numerous aggressions in the 1930s, which gave ample evidence of their plans for continuing conquest: Japan invaded Manchuria (1931, 1937), Italy crushed Abyssinia, or Ethiopia (1934), Franco suppressed republican freedom in Spain during the civil war there (1936–39), and Hitler absorbed Austria and Czechoslovakia (1938–39).

The simplified version of history, imbued with hindsight, suggests that everyone knew these bullies had to be stood up to and that the sooner that happened, the easier it would be to defeat them. Supposedly, it was obvious that conquest made the dictators more confident and strong, as they drew resources for warmaking, such as oil and steel, from the territories they overran. Looking back, 1940s veteran Roger Hilsman said, "World War II was a 'good' war. Hitler was a maniacal monster and, young as we were, we saw this and understood its implications" (Hilsman, 1).

The fly in the ointment, according to this argument, was that political leaders in the major democracies spinelessly dithered, trying to tolerate what the aggressors were doing, hoping they would be appeased by moderate expansion. These appeasers were led by Britain and France, the strongest free nations of

Europe. We are told that their heel-dragging approach was particularly reprehensible because they were partially responsible for the situation through the Treaty of Versailles (1919). At Versailles, they had placed the legal blame for World War I on Germany and its allies, inflicting the customary penalties, and allowing Hitler to feed off the hatred this engendered in Germany. Only in 1939, when the dictators had maximized their strength, did Britain and France acknowledge the need to fight, at least a year too late.

As with most myth, there is substantial truth here. But it is not the whole truth, and it distorts through simplification. This was not a clear-cut struggle between the forces of light and darkness; developments facing statesmen were the result of complex historical forces that added up to no simple picture. The right course of action was not as clear as it may seem now, when much of the complexity has been skimmed away by popularizers. The precise time to stand up to authoritarianism was not obvious. Nor were the dictator nations a monolith with a united front that prompted a uniform response. For instance, until the mid-1930s, Italy sometimes sided with Britain and France against Germany. It can be argued that the democracies gained strength by waiting to fight until 1939, instead of the earlier thirties. For example, Italy, the first state to embrace dictatorship and rearmament, hit its military peak sometime in the early thirties. By 1939, much of its equipment, including tanks and aircraft, was obsolete, whereas Britain's war machine, designed during later rearmament, was closer to state of the art when fighting began.

The idea that Hitler could somehow have been contained and made to behave by confronting him earlier is an argument more often asserted than proved; we are rarely told exactly how this would have worked militarily. The Munich conference of 1938 is often singled out as *the* craven moment when the march of aggression could have been halted, and later politicians have frequently referenced it to show we should never try to negotiate with regimes whose policies we oppose. But the outcome of going to war in 1938 is problematical, not certain. Moreover, although "appeasement" is blamed for causing World War II, we need to note emphatically that such a policy was tried only in Europe, not the Pacific. In Asia, where U.S. thinking dominated policy, the Allies followed a campaign of forceful "deterrence." Yet, it also failed, as the Japanese attacks of December 1941 on Pearl Harbor and elsewhere attest.

In short, there were no easy answers, no pat solutions. The history of international affairs in this period is complex and often seems daunting. But the satisfaction is in coming to understand why popular simplifications do not work as explanations of what happened and why.

The historical roots of World War II go back well before the 1919 Treaty of Versailles, certainly to the late eighteenth century, when opposing theories about the nature of the state and of citizenship came into conflict. One view supposed that people were basically rational and capable of self-government. This position stressed individual liberties and pointed toward liberal democracy. The counterargument held that self-government produced indecision and chaos: nations needed strong leaders, leaders with vision, to dictate policy. These contesting philosophies can be seen in the French Revolution of 1789, which began in liberalism and ended in the virtual dictatorship of Napoleon Bonaparte. For many nations, the choice between structures was still open in the twentieth century; they tended to vote democracy in good times and turn to strongmen in bad.

Also coming out of the eighteenth-century age of revolutions, both French and American, was a crucial connection between citizenship and soldiering. The rights to vote and to bear arms came to be aligned as mutual privileges of adult male membership in the body politic. The positive side of this connection meant that the citizen soldier could be called upon to defend the freedom of the state. The sinister side of the association between manhood and war fed the aggressive nationalism of the nineteenth century, pitting the massive armies of the major nations against one another.

This leads us to notice a paradox. The nineteenth century was a period of increasing material well-being, as industrial and agricultural innovations improved the standard of living. Yet, even as human comfort increased, an influential philosophy known as Social Darwinism (after the natural scientist Charles Darwin) held that in human affairs, as in nature, there is constant struggle and only the fittest survive. A nation must conquer or die. Ironically, then, the more a nation prospered, the more people worried they would become soft and a prey to their tougher, leaner neighbors. The answer lay in periodic bloodlettings to trim the fat and keep the nation alert.

In this perceived natural struggle, national expansion in search of resources was seen as key to survival. Western nations competed in subduing militarily weaker native peoples and turning their lands into colonies that provided the raw materials for Western industry, the markets for their finished goods, and occasional skirmishes to keep their young men on their mettle. This imperialism led to Western domination of much of the world. In Asia, only Japan stayed free of colonialism. This was important because, when in the twentieth century Japan was snubbed by the Western powers, it would take as its mission expelling the West from Asia. At the same time, the United States, pursuing its avenues of aggressive expansion, had by 1900 subdued its native population and was enlarging its dominance to include the Philippines plus other areas in the Pacific. This made it an inevitable rival to Japan for hegemony in that region, and the power struggle led directly to the Pacific war of 1941–45.

A Europe that increasingly defined individual masculine identity and the collective national character through combat reached its fulfillment in the World

War of 1914–18. Among the results of that mighty upheaval was the destruction of four imperial dynasties. Their demise created an unstable world situation: with the smashing of established institutions and the concomitant loss of a sense of structure and safety in people's lives, insecurity became a major political factor. Further destabilization favored the rise of strongmen, who would offer release from the fear of anarchy in return for the surrender of individual freedom and international understanding. Between 1917 and 1936, eleven European states chose dictatorship.

In the east, the Ottoman empire, which had sided with the unsuccessful Central Powers in World War I, fell apart. From its corpse, independent countries emerged, some of which, like Iraq, were artificial conglomerates of competing ethnic groups. As we know, the problems created then continue to plague the Middle East today, as nations still struggle to shape their identities. The Western powers, partly to protect their interests in the region, acted as midwives in the birth of these new nations. Britain, in particular, was involved, adding oversight of a large region, including a new Jewish homeland in Palestine, to its list of imperial obligations. British preoccupation with overseas problems would help to distract attention from the growing menace of Hitler.

In 1917, the retrogressive and inefficient czarist regime in Russia fell to a series of increasingly radical revolutions, culminating in the Bolshevik state. The Bolsheviks antagonized the Western Allies by fully withdrawing Russia from World War I and by their militant advocacy of world revolution, which drove them into isolation. Britain and the United States sent expeditionary forces to fight alongside the white Russian armies trying to overthrow the Communist regime, further deepening the mutual hostility. Russia was initially denied membership in the postwar League of Nations. Fear of Communist revolution would help to foster right-wing movements in Germany, Italy, and Spain. And distrust of Josef Stalin's increasingly ruthless, authoritarian state would further alienate statesmen in the democracies, preventing a common front against Hitler and therefore encouraging appeasement.

The Austro-Hungarian empire collapsed in 1918, leading to the creation of a potpourri of states in central and southern Europe. Some of these had a weak national identity and a questionable economic or military ability to sustain themselves. Among these was Czechoslovakia, a nation divided by ethnicity. Europe emerged from the war with twenty-seven separate currencies and 12,500 miles of new frontier. This was a patchwork situation, fluid and uncertain, guaranteeing that statesmen in the interwar years would not find straightforward solutions to complex questions of territorial sovereignty.

Finally, the German empire ended with the abdication of Kaiser Wilhelm II. Yet not all the factors in Germany's situation were negative. Renouncing the militarism of the imperial government, Germany moved to the liberal democracy of the Weimar Republic. At the peace treaty negotiations, France, whose northern territories had been the battleground for the western front, wanted large German concessions, including substantial territory, as compensation. And it wished Germany's industrial base dismantled so it could not rebuild a war machine to again invade France as it had in 1870 and 1914. Both the United States and Britain opposed these extreme demands. Germany's armed forces were limited in size, and the Rhineland was demilitarized to provide a buffer zone against further aggression, but at the same time, Germany's industrial resources in the Ruhr were reserved to it. In fact, both in population and industrial power, loser Germany remained potentially stronger than victor France.

Right-wing German nationalists later claimed that the Versailles treaty put all guilt for the war on the Reich. This was technically true: Article 231 of the treaty placed legal liability for the war on Germany and its allies. But the intent was not to brand Germany with all the moral guilt: the article was a prerequisite required to allow a legal basis for reparations. In fact, although reparations were asked for to compensate the victors for their losses, these were more moderate than Germany intended to extract if it had won. And such reparations traditionally were paid by the loser; they implied nothing more than that Germany had been beaten. Moreover, Britain and France had little choice in asking for reparations: they had borrowed heavily from America to fight the war, and America, acting on the traditional economic principle that foreign debts must be honored, demanded repayment. So, Britain and France had to go to Germany for the money.

In 1924, the reparations were put on a seemingly stable footing through the Dawes Plan, the work of an international committee headed by American Charles G. Dawes. It made German installments to the Allies feasible through American loans. The plan had merit, but it relied on American willingness to supply loans and German ability to afford them through international trade, particularly with America. Should this cycle of prosperity falter, there were disgruntled men waiting in the wings to topple the Weimar government in Germany.

Who were the angry and alienated? First, Germany had made the mistake of leaving largely intact the imperial military and administrative elite, many of whom despised democracy. This elite was loosely associated with various right-wing groups, including the militant Freikorps, literally "free corps," or freelance troops of veterans, paramilitaries who were self-appointed violent defenders of German honor. The extremists had two major objectives. First, they were determined to fight and destroy the Communists, who would align Germany with Bolshevik Russia. Second, they sought to overturn the Treaty of Versailles because they rejected the idea that Germany had been defeated in World War I and that it should make reparations. Because Allied forces had not marched deep into Germany when the war ended, reactionaries maintained that the army had not been broken but "stabbed in the back" by liberal politicians, who had panicked and sold out.

Freikorpsmen joined other nationalists in abhorring the postwar scattering of Germans. Though Germany remained largely intact, provinces taken from France and other neighbors in the nineteenth century were given back. The port of Danzig and a strip of territory connecting it to the new state of Poland were ceded, cutting East Prussia off from the rest of Germany. Also divorced from the fatherland were the Germans living in Austria and in the Sudeten region of Czechoslovakia.

The determination to repudiate Germany's defeat, to destroy communism, and to bring all German-speaking people into one national fold provided the basis for the right-wing opposition to Weimar. The Freikorpsmen, along with many other veterans, refused to accept the end of the war and the new world it had brought. Coming to maturity in the trenches, they saw life as war and peace as preparation for war. Said one Freikorps veteran: "People told us that the War was over. That made us laugh. We ourselves are the War. Its flame burns strongly in us. It envelops our whole being and fascinates us with the enticing urge to destroy" (Theweleit, 16).

The Weimar government was able to defend itself against these right-wing authoritarians only so long as it could deliver on the promise of prosperity. But, in 1922–23, the government devalued its currency to make reparation payments easier, and the consequent inflation hurt ordinary people, who found their savings almost worthless. Eventually, it took thousands of marks to buy a loaf of bread. Though the Dawes Plan ameliorated this situation, the confidence of ordinary Germans in capitalist democracy had been undermined. When, in 1929–30, a further economic catastrophe occurred, they turned readily to Adolf Hitler, a charismatic leader who promised an end to the capitalist cycle of boom and bust. Hitler shared the right-wing program of the Freikorps, and many of the Freikorps would serve in his National Socialist street-fighting units, called the SA or storm troopers. Like them, Hitler was obsessed by Versailles, but his regime was made possible partly by the Great Crash of 1929.

Ironically, perhaps some victor nations came out of World War I less satisfactorily than Germany. Although Britain and France had defended successfully their democratic way of life, it was at enormous cost in blood and treasure. Both were in debt. France faced a still-strong Germany on its borders and had lost a key ally, Russia, hunkered in hostile isolation. Britain's economic power was undermined, yet its imperial obligations increased. Throughout the interwar period, its politicians struggled with how to manage on resources inadequate to the demands of its great power role.

British statesmen believed their situation was made more complex by fluctuations in American policy. Without the sure backing of the United States, Britain was reluctant to take a firm leadership role in Europe. At the end of World War I, President Woodrow Wilson was a key exponent of international cooperation and the League of Nations, but the U.S. Senate voted against joining it in 1920, hurting the League's credibility.

Despite rejecting the League of Nations, America took steps to encourage peace in the 1920s, sponsoring conferences on arms limitation. But the public feared binding treaty commitments that might threaten American autonomy and perhaps trap the United States in a further foreign war. Many Americans had a legitimate distrust of European political stability. Millions had left Europe recently to find a new life in America and rejected entanglements with the Old World. As late as 1940, 11.5 million white Americans were first-generation immigrants, and a further 23 million were second-generation, out of a rough total of 118 million whites. They tended to favor letting Europe work out its own problems, and they put America first in a policy often labeled pejoratively as "isolationism."

Then, too, many American soldiers who went to France in 1917 and 1918 had been disillusioned by their reception. Expecting to be hailed as saviors, they were often treated as loud, vulgar intruders. They in turn found Europeans, except the Germans, dirty, backward, and unjustifiably arrogant. Like many returning American veterans before and after them, they brought back word that everything was much better at home. So many Americans soured on the idealism of the international crusade and turned to the pleasures of business as usual.

The result was that American foreign policy tended to lack authority and, at times, consistency. Americans were willing to give the world an example of peaceful cooperation in an international capitalist system, but they stopped short of a commitment to ensure that such a system was not undermined. The confusion was made worse by Europeans' failure to understand the American political system. For example, in Britain the head of the legislative branch (Parliament) is also the chief executive (prime minister), and so the two branches of government speak with one voice. In America the distribution of powers means that the legislative branch (Congress) and the executive branch (president) may well disagree, as they did over League membership and, later, support for Britain and France. This division could lead to giving out mixed signals and to stalemate on policy formulation.

In the United States, domestic concerns and foreign policy did not always dovetail. America insisted that the Europeans pay back their war debts, but in 1922 they passed a restrictive tariff on imported goods, making it hard for the debtor nations to earn the dollars to pay back their loans. Similarly, loans from

America were pivotal to Germany's ability to make reparations payments. Yet the federal government put no guarantees behind the Dawes Plan, so that when, in 1927 and 1928, the stock market offered more lucrative opportunities for investors, the flow of crucial dollars to Germany decreased.

As speculation on Wall Street became wilder, stock prices doubled in two years, a growth without solid foundation. The federal government did little to curb speculative fever. The economy went into recession, and sagging public confidence led to the 1929 stock market crash. Dependence on American dollars meant the crash affected all major nations and led some to determine that their economic safety lay in international conquest, not cooperation. Americans had genuinely hoped for an era of peace and prosperity, but the unregulated free-market system and their reluctance to be obligated abroad meant they could not guide events in the direction they wanted.

Finally, the United States, along with the other democracies, did not pursue a consistent policy toward aggressor nations. In Europe, it continued to trade with dictators—even though it asked them to behave. In the Pacific, by contrast, America felt threatened by the expansion of Japan, and succeeding administrations cold-shouldered the Japanese, pressuring the British to do likewise. As Japan went from friend to enemy, Britain felt compelled to compensate by seeking some accommodation with Italy and Germany, a dilemma critics of British appeasement policies usually failed to acknowledge.

The two victor nations most uncomfortable in the postwar world were Italy and Japan. Italy had lost 600,000 and experienced indifferent success in the fighting. In 1917, its army was badly beaten by Austria in the debacle of Caporetto, a disaster vividly described in Ernest Hemingway's *A Farewell to Arms* (1929). In return for suffering and humiliation, Italy expected rich rewards at Versailles in the form of strategic territories from the defeated powers. But the major Allies rejected much of its request and gave only what Benito Mussolini referred to contemptuously as the crumbs of rich colonial pickings. In 1922, when the powers set treaty limits to naval strength, Italy was restricted to the same sized Mediterranean fleet as Britain, a sea that Italy justifiably saw as its own. Though the arrangement was to protect strategic British oil supplies, Italian nationalists perceived it as a further humiliation.

To make matters worse, the country entered peace with a depressed economy and high unemployment, particularly among returning veterans, whose dissatisfaction was a hotbed for revolution. Bloody industrial strikes convinced conservatives that Communists could seize Italy. Fearful, shocked, they embraced a strong leader who offered renewed national pride and economic and social stability in return for the surrender of democratic freedoms. This was not hard for many people, who held liberals responsible for Italy's situation.

The strongman was Mussolini, who took authority in 1922 as Il Duce, "the Chief." To the slow and complicated operations of democracy, Mussolini opposed the perceived decisiveness of the man of will and force. "Mussolini is always right," said a poster. Il Duce undercut communism by promising an end to labor-management disputes: workers were guaranteed employment and fringe benefits, such as paid vacations, in return for passivity. How would resources-short Italy pay for prosperity? It would take the lands and raw materials denied it at Versailles. Mussolini, the charismatic military chief, would recreate the Mediterranean empire of Rome (hence *fascism*, from the fasces, or bundles of sticks, carried in Roman processions).

Fascism fostered the cult of personality, the image of the great man in whose hands you could safely leave your burdens. This idea of safety was attractive to many veterans and others bewildered by postwar instability. In an insecure and hostile world, the flag-waving and chest-beating of fascism gave a comforting, if often false, sense of collective strength and direction. Mussolini made the trains run on time was the popular boast.

In fact, Mussolini did not exert the total power attributed to him; both the king, Victor Emmanuel III, and the pope, Pius XI, remained as competing authority figures. And fascism never achieved the efficient regulation of society claimed for it; labor unrest continued, and behind the facade of the new society, many Italians slipped into poverty. Their plight was unknown because fascist control of the media put only the regime's successes before the public. And those who might challenge the official line were either liquidated or intimidated into silence. Newsreels showcased Italy's crack fighting units, concealing that some troops were poorly equipped and low in morale. Fascism's flashy surface impressed other Europeans and led Hitler to copy its techniques.

Japan began rising to world power status toward the end of the nineteenth century, when it emerged as the one independent Asian nation with a recognizably modern business-industrial base. Like Italy, Japan was short of resources and sought to offset this deficit by expanding at the expense of its neighbors, especially China. The latter, in the second half of the nineteenth century, was a weak nation exploited for profit by the imperialist states. These demanded special trading rights and "concessions," or reserved territories where they had privileged access to markets and raw materials. For Japan, a share of the Chinese pie seemed requisite for economic power. The United States, favoring equal marketing opportunities for all and an end to the imperial system through its Open Door policy, strongly opposed concessions and would eventually come into conflict with Japan in its attempt to make China an economically dependent province.

Japan startled the world by easily defeating imperial Russia in the war of 1904–05. This gave it a good foothold in Manchuria, China's northern province, formerly under Russian influence. In World War I, Japan, on the winning side and closely allied to Britain, expected, like Italy, to do well in the division of spoils. But it, too, was disappointed. During the war, it had captured the German concession in China's northern Shandong province, along with other territory along the Pacific coast. It felt entitled to be recognized as the major power in the western Pacific and the premier influence in China. But it was snubbed at Versailles, where Japan's request for a statement supporting the racial equality of all nations was rejected. Japan was not seen as a full partner by the Western nations. Also, the United States championed the future national autonomy of China and pressured Japan to give up its conquests there.

To the prideful Japanese, the Washington naval treaty of 1921–22, cutting their fleet to three-fifths the size of the American and British navies, was also offensive. The treaty, however, was not unreasonable, as it made Japan paramount in the Pacific; unlike the other powers, it did not also have to keep a naval presence in other oceans. But the Japanese felt the ratio implied inferior status. At the same time, in 1922, the U.S. Supreme Court, in the first of several racial decisions, declared Japanese ineligible for citizenship. In 1923, a harsh ruling upheld California and Washington state laws denying Japanese the right to own property. In 1924, the barriers were completed with the Exclusion Act, virtually banning Asian immigration.

Though these measures boded ill for future relations, Japan and America did try to work together, particularly through trade. Japan offered appeasement by withdrawing substantial forces from China and cutting its military budget. It acquiesced in the territorial integrity of China. But this cooperation was based on the premise that Japan could relinquish expansion and still prosper by increasing trade with America. During most of the twenties, this worked. Japan's industrial production doubled, and exports boomed, with 40 percent going to the United States. Yet there were ominous signs. Japanese liberal politicians and businessmen, forces for moderation, were opposed by extreme elements in the officer corps. Arrogant and feudal in outlook, these officers played a major role in Japanese politics, and they aspired to conquest. China, struggling to throw off colonial status, took back many of its concessions and moved to enforce uniform administration of the provinces. Some Japanese statesmen and soldiers feared that an independent China under American influence might deny them raw materials and markets.

In 1929, Wall Street crashed. During the next two years, world trade declined by one-third, and Japanese exports fell by the same amount. The price of raw silk, a staple commodity, plummeted 65 percent in one year. Workers' standard of living was cut by 33 percent. Small farmers and businessmen suffered, infuriating many in the army, which drew from this class to fill the ranks. In 1930, America tried to help its own depressed industries through the Smoot-Hawley tariff, which raised barriers on imported goods by 50 percent. The United States, with abundant natural resources and domestic markets, could perhaps afford to close its doors to the outside world and weather the depression alone. The Japanese could not.

The experience convinced some Japanese leaders to seek self-sufficiency through conquest. Their first target was again China. In 1931, the army command in Manchuria attacked, under the pretext of alleged depredations of Japanese property. The home government endorsed the move, and by 1932 the Japanese had sufficient control to rename the region Manchukuo, a puppet state. Although Japan charged Chinese provocation, its aggression was condemned by the League of Nations. Japan left the League and ultimately came into loose alliance with Italy and Germany, defining themselves as have-not nations, needing to meet their needs by conquest. Japanese leaders who saw the fatal error in this policy would be either assassinated by army militants or intimidated into silence.

The financial crash and resulting Great Depression undercut the democracies' ability to show that capitalism could bring prosperity and security to all nations through the mutual benefits of trade. As the breadlines grew, so did the fear that the despairing would turn to communism or foment anarchy. Faced with that threat, more than one country embraced strongmen, promising a restoration of stability. The most important of these was Der Führer (the Leader), Hitler.

The fiscal meltdown and global depression hit Germany hard, being dependent on American loans, which dried up in the monetary crisis. Also, Germany lacked thirty-three of thirty-five raw materials deemed essential for industrial production. Its goods had to be sold abroad to earn the money to buy these foreign commodities, but as country after country protected their home markets to help their internal industrial recovery, Germany found its export trade collapsing. With additional stagnation, caused by an agricultural glut, Germany's prosperity crumbled, and by 1932, 6 million were unemployed.

The nazi movement, cashing in on the misery, did well in the 1930 elections, becoming the second largest political party. As succeeding chancellors (prime ministers) proved incapable of ending the depression, Hitler inevitably became the "available man" and was chosen as chancellor in January 1933. Having gained power by democratic means, the Nazis now moved to end genuine representative government. A fire in the Reichstag, or parliament building, possibly set by a crank, became Hitler's pretext for claiming Germany faced a vast international Jewish-communist conspiracy, virtually amounting to a state of war. In the crisis, Hitler demanded emergency dictatorial powers, which he subsequently used to end political opposition. Germany became a one-party state. The Third Reich, which Hitler boasted would last a thousand years, had begun.

We might say simply that at this point Germany had opted to put its future in the hands of a madman. But how could this be? Then it would follow that a majority of Germans were also insane. When we think about it, such an idea does not help us understand what happened, so we must seek a better diagnosis. Hitler was not mad in any conventional sense. Rather, he grasped the nature of forces at work in his time and sought to control them for his violent vision of a greater, racially purified Germany.

Hitler was primarily a nationalist who shared with many Germans a faith in their country's destiny for world power. He believed the Treaty of Versailles had outrageously hamstrung German potential and must be repudiated. Germans living in Austria or Czechoslovakia should be repatriated to the Reich. Assertive nationalism was not unique to Germany. Pride in country and competition between countries marked the modern period, replacing earlier loyalties to broader human allegiances, such as the medieval concept of a united Christendom. In repudiating Versailles, ending reparations, and rearming Germany, Hitler was intelligible to his countrymen and to politicians in other countries who claimed the same rehabilitation for their peoples fifteen years after the war.

In imposing his will on German society, Hitler showed outstanding ability in two areas: first, as a dedicated soldier and, second, as a master politician who understood completely the importance of image in winning the modern audience. These twin foundations of success were noted by one of Hitler's generals, Field Marshal von Brauchitsch, who said in 1938 that Der Führer combined in his person the epitome of both the soldier and the National Socialist, the warrior and consummate manipulator.

Hitler had a mediocre career as a commercial artist in Vienna before finding his identity in the trenches of World War I. He wrote in his book, *Mein Kampf,* that, compared to this gigantic struggle, all events that had gone before receded into insignificance. Hitler won two Iron Crosses for valor and decided that life is war, a struggle to see who is fit to survive. He became a Social Darwinist of a simple and dangerous kind, dedicated to German success through adopting military values and goals. "Those who want to live, let them fight, and those who do not want to fight in this world of eternal struggle do not deserve to live" (Hitler, 289).

Deeply impressed by Italian fascism, he grafted its leading qualities onto nazism. He inculcated obedience to a leader in his disciplined followers, whose muscle was used to terrorize or liquidate opponents. These included communists and trades union leaders, whose organizations were suppressed. In return for an end to organized labor, business leaders pledged allegiance to nazism and became its tool in rearmament. Terror became an everyday aspect of government. Erich Maria Remarque, whose antiwar books were banned by the Nazis, wrote that distrust and fear of betrayal to the authorities permeated life under the Third Reich. Nobody felt safe and it became axiomatic to keep your mouth shut. Even the private Nazi army, the SA brownshirts, were kept in line by terror. Hitler, suspecting their head, Ernst Roehm, of wanting to replace him, ordered his bodyguard of SS blackshirts to eliminate SA leaders in the "night of the long knives," June 30, 1934. The regular army approved, perceiving the SA as threatening its position; it now threw its power to Hitler.

Brownshirts, blackshirts, jackboots, flags, parades: in creating public images of nazism, Hitler the showman tapped into people's craving for spectacle. He understood jobs and creature comforts fulfill only part of human longings; people also want excitement, a cause bigger and more colorful than daily work offers, to give drama and higher purpose to living. Due to industrial standardization on the production line, conformity in clothing and behavior demanded by the modern milieu, life seemed monotonous yet also tense and unstable in a shifting political economy. Nazism brought pageantry to daily life, the allure of military display. Hitler was impressed by American marching bands and copied their style. Nazis adapted the Harvard chant, "Fight, Fight, Fight," to "Sieg Heil, Sieg Heil."

In one sense, nazism was good entertainment. American journalist William L. Shirer understood that Hitler "is restoring pageantry and color and mysticism to the drab lives of twentieth-century Germans" (Shirer, 18). A German woman recalled years later, "I loved the constant marching and singing, with flags and bunting everywhere. I wanted to join the League of German girls" (Engelmann, 27). Nazism particularly appealed to adolescents, who needed to fit in and be affirmed by the group while feeling special at the same time. Nazi youth organizations gave teenagers a prestige rare in their culture; some even got to beat up unpopular teachers and other resented adult authority figures.

Hitler grasped that many people want political leaders to simplify complex issues for them. The masses, he said, are weak; they want to be led. He admired American and British advertising campaigns that reduced thoughts to sound bites. Nazi propaganda minister Joseph Goebbels sold the party as Madison Avenue sold soap powder. This was perhaps vulgar but still intelligible to foreign politicians. But should not the Nazis' treatment of Jews, Gypsies, Communists, intellectuals, liberals, homosexuals, and other "undesirables" have signaled the sickness of the movement to the West? Not necessarily. Prejudice ran deep in most European societies: nationalism itself could be a put-down of outsiders, and anti-Semitism was widespread. The British empire rested on assumed white superiority over non-Aryan peoples.

But, we ask, is there a matter of degree here, a line beyond which persecution is intolerable? Perhaps. But where was that line? It was not until 1941 that the Nazis undertook the "final solution" (large-scale extermination of undesirable groups of people). Throughout the 1930s, Hitler tried to get rid of Jews by deportation. Most Western nations accepted only a few, including the United States, which did not expand immigration quotas. The outside world assumed that Jews trapped in Germany went to concentration camps merely to undergo "reeducation." After the embarrassment of Allied propaganda in World War I, which falsely portrayed Germans as baby killers and nun rapers, people balked at believing stories of Nazi atrocities.

Also, an accepted principle of international law in the 1930s held that a nation might imprison or otherwise discipline domestic problem elements; the international community should not encroach on this aspect of sovereignty. Only after World War II was this axiom challenged, great powers now asserting a right to initiate regime change in weaker nations and subsequently rebuilding them in the victor's image. (This claim to nation-building following preemptive war was forcefully advanced by President George W. Bush's administration, particularly with regard to Iraq under Saddam Hussein.)

By 1942, the concentration camps had become slaughterhouses for millions, but they were originally detention centers, political prisons based on foreign models. Britain, during the Boer War (1899–1902), had used such camps to restrain hostile elements of the South African population. So did Spain and America in the Philippines. The ultimate mass murder in the camps correctly shocks us as madness. But it was a special madness, born of the twentieth-century experience. Hitler endured World War I, in which 13 million soldiers were killed and in which death was organized along modern management principles, carried out on an industrial scale previously unimaginable. In Hitler's mind, if the best elements of society, fine young men, could be slaughtered legally in this way, then why not undesirable and criminal elements? For a military veteran, large-scale butchery could appear a normal aspect of life.

Some English-speaking politicians were sympathetic to Hitler's racial theories, emphasizing the superiority of northern European or Germanic stock. They found his bullying methods uncouth and his theatricals tawdry but hoped he could be worked with and that his approach to governing would moderate as the regime matured. They responded sympathetically to his attacks on communism, which Hitler detested as a raising up of the stupid many at the expense of the gifted few. He drew support from conservatives like Geoffrey Dawson, editor of the influential London *Times*, and American newspaper baron William Randolph Hearst. A major factor in the democracies' attempt to accommodate Hitler was their perception of Germany as a military bulwark against Soviet expansion. Some hoped Hitler would attack Russia and the two systems might exhaust each other. Fear of Soviet ambitions fed tolerance of nazism. Hitler said, in 1937, "The English will get under the same eiderdown with me; in their politics they follow the same guidelines as I do, namely, the overriding necessity to annihilate Bolshevism" (Toland, 448).

Then, too, at a time when many countries were mired in economic stagnation, nazism seemed to have put Germany on the road to recovery. By 1935, the country appeared prosperous, with money for public works like the new auto-bahns (superhighways). Hitler raised the quality of workers' lives through vaca-tions, health care benefits, public parks and other free recreational facilities, plus a modestly priced automobile, the Volkswagen, or "people's car." The list was impressive, although we now know much seeming prosperity was illusory, and nazism was less efficient than its public image.

Progress was, in fact, based upon using stockpiled natural resources and pour-ing public money into the arms industry. But the resources had to be replaced for the prosperity to grow. They could be paid for through exports or taken by force. As Hitler had no faith in international markets after the 1929 crash, it made sense to use the new armaments to take materials by force. These resources could then be used to produce more guns for more conquest. By 1936, Germany was on a war path. Hitler demanded lebensraum, living space, for his surplus pop-ulation, to prevent future unemployment and provide resources for Germany's factories. He would get this space from the east, from Russia. But first, he would unite the German-speaking peoples of western Europe.

We have looked at how three key states—Italy, Japan, and Germany—came to define themselves as have-nots, lacking the natural resources and trading power of such "haves" as the United States and the British empire. We must now ex-amine how developments came to end in war, asking why hostilities began in 1939 rather than earlier.

To begin with, the 1931 Japanese invasion of Manchuria did not go unnoticed. The British held extensive interests in Asia. Since World War I, the annual im-perial defense budget had been planned on the assumption that there would not be a major war for ten years. In 1931, this idea was scrapped. But, ironically, at-tention to Asia led Britain to be cautious in Europe, for it no longer had the mili-tary strength to fight a three-ocean war: in the Pacific against Japan, in the Med-iterranean against Italy, and in the Atlantic against Germany. British overseas dominions, powerful on paper, were in fact dubious assets. Australia did not have the population base or industrial resources to defend itself alone against Japan. India was in turmoil over home rule. Canada, South Africa, and Ulster did not want to fight anywhere. In short, Britain's loss of Japan's friendship created sig-nificant problems. The United States, less respectful of Japan, also became pre-occupied with the Pacific after 1931. But America, like Britain, did not want war over Manchuria, and indeed, the United States continued for a period to sell war matériel to all the belligerents.

In 1934, Mussolini embarked on his African empire by attacking Abyssinia. Was this the time for the democracies to fight? A war might have stopped Mus-solini, but it would have left Hitler untouched. Italy had attacked a "native" or colored people. Though some Western states were moving away from naked colonialism, both the French and British still had substantial interests in Africa, and it would have appeared two-faced to fight Italy. For France, the problem was compounded by fear of a revived Germany. France and Italy shared a border. Should they cease to be friends, Italy could stab its neighbor across that border while France was fighting Germany. This fear was realized in 1940, when Italy joined in Germany's war, hastening France's collapse. Britain wanted no conflict in the Mediterranean, and many leading citizens (including, for a while, Winston Churchill) respected Mussolini's energy and opposition to communism.

Nevertheless, the democracies did not aid Italy's invasion and led the League of Nations in passing economic sanctions on the aggressor. Unfortunately, the sanctions had the unforeseen effect of driving Italy closer to Germany. Hitler, who had already rejected League membership, continued to supply Italy with war materials. Mussolini had doubts about nazism, particularly its anti-Semitism, which had no place in fascism. But he now felt obliged to cultivate Germany.

American actions were not always helpful. The United States weakened the embargo by continuing to trade with Italy; its oil exports fueled the fascist war machine. President Franklin D. Roosevelt declared his moral disapproval of Mussolini but, needing the Italian-American vote with an election coming up, went no further. As late as 1940, 80 percent of U.S. Italian-language newspapers were pro-Mussolini, arguing that he had elevated Italy's power and prosperity. In short, the attack on Abyssinia alienated Italy from the democracies without a compensating gain. But what else might have happened? Was there an easy answer for any politician at this moment?

Perhaps a better place to stand against authoritarianism was in Spain during the civil war of 1936–39 when right-wing forces under General Francisco Franco overthrew the republic, helped by German and Italian troops. Martha Gellhorn, an American war correspondent who covered Spain, believed that the democracies became morally bankrupt when they left the republic to its fate. The republican cause made war respectable again among liberals previously alienated by the seemingly pointless butchery of World War I. Ernest Hemingway saluted the republican forces in *For Whom the Bell Tolls* (1940). Yet the situation was complicated: this was not simply a struggle between good and evil. Many on the left were antidemocratic, crudely anti-Catholic, backward looking, and as brutal as their enemies. After Russia sent troops to Spain, the republican cause came under authoritarian Soviet domination, and many more moderate democratic leaders were liquidated.

Conversely, not all right-wingers were fascists; some were only conservative nationalists. Business interests in the United States and Britain feared that the republicans would nationalize their Spanish assets and that the Soviets would dominate Spain if the republicans won. Franco seemed a safer bet. The Firestone Corporation celebrated his victories with ads saying that the general and their tires were both winners. Further, American Catholics resented republican persecution of the church. In short, the democracies were too internally divided to fight. Anyway, the problem ultimately was Hitler, not Franco.

In 1936, German forces remilitarized the Rhineland, the buffer zone with France. French politicians considered fighting, but neither French nor British generals felt they could win an offensive war. France's economy had slipped badly during the Great Depression, and there was no money to replace obsolete industrial plants. Consequently, the armed forces lacked modern tanks and long-range bombers needed for an attack on Germany. Between 1933 and 1937, France produced only one-tenth as many military aircraft as Germany. World War I was still unpopular in France, so that while there was peacetime conscription, draftees could not be kept long enough to train them for offensive operations. They were prepared only to garrison static defensive positions, especially the concrete and steel fortresses of the Maginot Line, which stretched across northern France. Britain had the Royal Navy, but it could send only two army divisions to France, fewer than it had dispatched in 1914, and the Royal Air Force also was only just receiving modern planes.

Some have argued that the democracies merely needed to exhibit a show of force, because Hitler would have backed down in face of a resolute policy. This is debatable. Hitler cast himself as the man of iron will, and his operational orders made clear that German forces would withdraw only to defensive positions on the Rhine before turning to fight. From the democracies' perspective, the longer they had to rearm, the better. Anyway, there was some sympathy for the Germans: wasn't the Rhineland German after all? At this point, there was still a hope that the international order could be stabilized by accepting a moderate revision of the map drawn at Versailles.

From 1934 on, Hitler carried out a campaign of intimidation and propaganda to undermine the government of neighboring Austria, and in March 1938, his troops occupied that country during the Anschluss. Europe now became distinctly uneasy because, with the added population and resources of Austria, Germany significantly increased its offensive potential. Hitler had netted five army divisions, iron ore and oil, and $200 million in gold and other reserves. Many people understood for the first time the real threat to European peace the Nazis posed. Yet uncertainty remained: Austrians were predominantly of Germanic stock, and many of them welcomed Der Führer, a native son. Was it not reasonable for this ethnic group to wish unification with Germany?

Hitler used the same pretext to demand the Sudetenland province of Czechoslovakia, with a German population of 3.25 million. He claimed, with some justification, that Germans had been discriminated against by the Czechoslovakian state, denied equal access to education, jobs, and public funding. The tension led to the Munich conference of September 1938. Here, without properly consulting Czechoslovakia, Britain and France gave in to Hitler's demands.

Why did Britain and France not stand up to Hitler? They still felt unprepared for offensive war, and they feared German counterattack. To comprehend this, we must understand the claims made by the air forces of the Western nations between the wars. Out of sincere belief, and to gain funding for their services, they asserted that air power alone would win the next war. Rather than stalemate and butchery in the bloody muck of trench warfare, bombers would fly deep into enemy territory and bomb its cities into submission. One proponent of air power was Billy Mitchell in the United States. He used filmed sequences of bomber attacks on such targets as old battleships to convince the public that control of the skies was crucial to national security.

The Germans and Italians also used film to give an inflated image of their air power. They were aided by celebrated American flyer Charles A. Lindbergh, touring Europe at this time. He was courted by public relations personnel from the Luftwaffe (German air force). In much publicized media statements, he pronounced the Luftwaffe the most powerful in Europe, followed by Italy's air fleet. The unreadiness of France appalled him. Shortly after the Munich conference, he announced that, had war come, the French could not have stopped the bombing of Paris. "There was not, and is not, in France one fighting plane as fast as the latest German bombers! The French air fleet is almost nonexistent from the standpoint of a modern war" (Lindbergh, 85–86).

Lindbergh thought the British were better off but still unready for combat. The prominent American flyer's views were digested by British ministers and fear of the Luftwaffe factored largely at Munich. When Prime Minister Neville Chamberlain flew home from the conference, he passed over thousands of British homes that at this point he believed could not be protected from air raids. Britain needed more time.

Also on Chamberlain's mind was the attitude of the United States, still struggling out of the Great Depression and disillusioned about the failure of the last war to bring lasting European peace. In 1934, a congressional committee headed by Senator Gerald P. Nye concluded that arms manufacturers had worked to get America into World War I. Understandably, a majority of Americans opposed committing troops to Europe. Moreover, Europe was remote, and many Americans did not understand the issues between the contending forces; for many, Joe Louis's fight to regain the world heavyweight boxing title was more interesting than Munich. President Roosevelt merely sent a telegram urging Hitler to settle the Sudeten question amicably.

Britain and France had one other possible ally, the Soviet Union, which was willing to guarantee Czechoslovakia's borders, a barrier against German expansion eastward. But Western statesmen did not trust Stalin's territorial ambitions. And Poland, which lay between Russia and Czechoslovakia, refused to let Soviet troops cross its territory for fear they would stay. Poland had grievances against Czechoslovakia for treating poorly its ethnics in that country and, in October, attacked its neighbor. This action underlines the dilemma facing Britain and France. Was Czechoslovakia a model democracy, as often claimed? Or was it an artificial fabrication, patched together from pieces of the Austro-Hungarian empire, a collection of warring ethnic groups, not worth a world war?

Whatever the case, Czechoslovakia suffered. It was forced to relinquish its fortified mountain frontier and other substantial territory that the Nazis would have paid heavily to obtain militarily. But this was not appeasement without a bottom line. Britain and France would go no further. In March 1939, Chamberlain warned Hitler that he could make no greater mistake than supposing he could dominate Europe by force without Britain resisting to the full extent of its power. Germany swallowed what remained of Czechoslovakia, and in April, Britain introduced peacetime conscription for the first time in its history. Hitler now demanded the end of the Polish corridor and the reunification of East Prussia with Germany. Britain and France guaranteed Poland's borders. When, on September 1, 1939, Germany attacked Poland, the democracies honored their pledges and fought.

In retrospect, it is puzzling that so much is made of Munich, since Britain and France made clear their intention to give no more to Hitler. Had they fought in 1938, there was a chance Czechoslovakia might have survived. But by waiting a year, Britain had the air power to win the Battle of Britain, British aircraft production overtaking Germany's in autumn 1939. And crucially, the new British air raid early warning system, radar, became operational, meaning that Fighter Command would confront the attackers and Nazi bombers would not always get through.

The West's flirtation with Hitler was unconscionable in many ways, especially in its cynicism regarding abuse of Jews and other Nazi victims. Also questionable was the toleration of Hitler's aggressiveness by some in the West who hoped that Germany would be a gun turned against Russia. Realizing belatedly that appeasement had failed, Britain and France made an eleventh-hour attempt to ally with Russia, but they could not accept Stalin's concurrent demand for expansion into Finland and the Baltic republics.

Any remaining hope of alliance collapsed when Stalin and Hitler, putting aside vast ideological differences, signed the Nazi-Soviet Nonaggression Pact in August 1939, stating that either power would remain neutral if the other went to war with a third party (i.e., they would not attack each other). This left Hitler free to invade Poland, as he would now face a war only in the west. A secret protocol of the pact agreed to divide up Poland, sealing that country's fate. Stalin mistakenly believed this agreement would cushion Russia against German aggression; Hitler's invasion of Russia in 1941 forced the Soviets to see their mistake and work with the Western Allies.

Developments in Europe helped shape Japanese policy. Into the 1930s, significant business and political elements in Japan still wanted to accommodate the Western powers and grow through commerce. But the success of Italy and Germany in taking resources by force played into the hands of Japan's war party. In the summer of 1937, the army launched a full-scale attack on China. This aggression particularly upset the United States, which had a genuine interest in Chinese independence, as well as strategic interests in Asia that were threatened. The extreme brutality of the Japanese military increased public outrage. A 1938 opinion poll showed that a majority of Americans favored military aid to China but not to Britain and France.

The Chinese nationalist leader, Chiang Kai-shek, and his wife were skilled diplomats, who made much of the so-called Tanaka memorandum. Supposedly written in 1927 by a Japanese minister, the memorandum was a blueprint for world conquest. It was used to stir up American feeling against Japan by playing on an old fear that Asian hordes, the "yellow peril," would swamp America through a military invasion across the Pacific. The document was later shown to be a forgery, but the threat to the region's stability was real enough.

In attacking China, Japan sought self-sufficiency through conquest. The war party believed that the alternative meant remaining a minor power, living on a resources-short and overpopulated land space. The attack signaled the defeat of liberal political and business forces that believed the nation could achieve prominence through peaceful economic competition. Liberals thought expansion would antagonize the United States and other Western powers on whom Japan depended for vital raw materials: in 1936 Japan bought one-third of its imports from America, including 66 percent of its oil; rubber and more oil came from British colonies; another 25 percent of its oil supply was from the Dutch East Indies. With China, these states made up the so-called ABCD powers. They would inevitably bring economic pressure on Japan, which could either back down or expand the war to get the resources it was denied.

In the spring of 1940, the United States sent the bulk of its Pacific fleet from the west coast to Hawaii in the hope of warning off Japan. In late July, 1940, economic sanctions were imposed, cutting off key war materials: aviation gasoline, lubricating oil, and military-grade scrap iron. And, in August, America made a defense agreement by which Britain got fifty destroyers to fight Hitler in return for Caribbean bases the U.S. Navy could use against Japan. Thus, the major powers in the Pacific moved steadily toward military confrontation.

Should Japan back down? In Europe, Germany and Italy were doing well: the French and Dutch had been defeated. Britain's back was to the wall, and America had to put some resources into helping that nation survive. With so many potential opponents in difficulty, Japan gambled on a war for hegemony in the western Pacific. The region would be liberated from Western imperialists, and Japan would assume a leading role as "the first among equals" in an Asian co-prosperity sphere. In September, the Tri-Partite Pact, a defensive alliance with Germany and Italy, was signed, and Japanese forces began their southward conquest, attacking northern French Indochina. France, in Hitler's pocket, could do little to resist. The United States responded with a total embargo on scrap iron. In November, the Chinese nationalists were given a $100 million loan to buy arms.

Events quickly came to a head. In July 1941, Japan swallowed southern Indochina. America froze all Japanese assets and imposed a total fuel oil embargo, as did Britain and Holland. U.S. B-17 bombers moved to Pacific bases. American officials warned Japan that the bombers could destroy the vulnerable wood and paper houses of Japanese cities, a threat intended to dissuade the Japanese from further aggression. But the Japanese military, convinced that America was preparing for an obliterating offensive war on the home islands, demanded a preemptive strike to seize the resources Japan needed and perhaps force the United States to formally divide power in the Pacific. From this perspective, Pearl Harbor was the last act in the degeneration of U.S.–Japanese relations.

At no time was there an attempt to appease Japan. Western politicians always assumed that an Asian nation could be made to back down. British foreign secretary Anthony Eden, echoing President Roosevelt's views, argued that a solid show of firmness was more likely to prevent than encourage Japanese aggression. In fact, the policy had the opposite effect. If appeasement failed in Europe, deterrence failed in Asia. There was no one conveniently applicable formula for solving international crises.

Looking back, the events of the period do not reflect particularly well on any major players. Yet their actions are intelligible if we are careful to delineate the full historical context in which they had to perform. Who is to say that if the world we know collapsed, as it did for millions after World War I and again in the Great Depression, we should act more wisely or be any better at finding the correct, workable solutions?

CHAPTER TWO

The Patterns of War, 1939–1945

In this chapter, I review the major courses and character of strategic operations in World War II. While it is understandable that, as a society, we should concentrate on the contributions of our own leadership and military actions, many other nations and cohesive groups took part in the conflict and contributed to the outcomes. The D-Day landings of June 1944 in Western Europe were indeed a pivotal moment in shifting momentum to the Allies, but we must recognize other vital watershed events, even if this means sharing credit with others, some of whom the United States ceased to see as friends during or after the war. Finally, although it is popular to see World War II as a conflict dominated by fast-moving, technologically advanced fighting machines operating in a lightning or blitzkrieg environment, the bulk of fighting, particularly in the later stages, was in fact a brutal slogging match, as ground troops ground their way forward in a destructive contest of attrition.

World War II began when Germany invaded Poland on September 1, 1939. Few experts gave the technically obsolete Polish military machine much chance of winning. But the speed and completeness of Germany's victory were startling. By September 14, German forces were in the rear of Poland's capital, Warsaw, and had completed a giant encircling movement, trapping the major Polish armies in a net to the north. By September 27, significant resistance by the outmaneu-vered and demoralized Polish forces had ended. Their defeat was due not only to older equipment, as the Germans, too, had their share of cavalry and horse-drawn transport. Hitler's forces introduced a new method of waging war: the blitzkrieg, or lightning attack.

The Polish undertook a conventional deployment that looked back to the patterns of World War I. Major armies were spread out in largely immobile defensive positions to protect as much as possible of Poland's northern provinces bordering Germany. Tanks were divided up piecemeal as supports to the infantry. Communication with reserves to the rear was largely by rail, a slow and easy target for air attack. Poland expected a slugging match on this broad front, lasting long enough for French and British military support to arrive. But Germany changed the nature of the battlefield, avoiding the necessity of meeting the bulk of Polish forces head-on and so achieving swift successes.

The Luftwaffe quickly took out opposing air defenses and then roamed at will between the Polish armies and their supports, severing rail communications and numbing ability to react. Tanks, instead of being squandered in small numbers, were concentrated in powerful panzer (armored) units, which brought overwhelming superiority to bear on weak spots in the enemy disposition, punching through into the rear. Conventional wisdom said the German forces should then stop and mop up. Instead, the panzers struck deep into the Polish heartland, sowing terror and defeatism, while German infantry behind them exploited the breakthrough to encircle and contain the enemy. Blocked from retreat and cut off from reinforcement, the emasculated Polish forces necessarily capitulated.

This innovative battle practice framed the contemporary image of World War II, a view encouraged by the Germans, whose newsreels showcased panzer attacks and downplayed glitches in execution. There was some truth to the characterization. But this kind of mobile warfare, in which relatively small forces captured huge territories quickly, primarily characterized the opening phases of the war, up through 1941. In this period, German (and Japanese forces) defeated opponents whose equipment was often obsolete and whose generals were wedded to past ideas. Ironically, however, both the Germans and Japanese took more territory than they could defend against powerful opponents if the conflict bogged down into a war of attrition. The Axis had neither the military nor economic forces to wage extended campaigns. They also faced stubborn resistance movements within conquered territories that tied down resources needed elsewhere on the front lines. If the Axis nations failed to reach an early compromise peace with their enemies, based on their gains, their ultimate defeat was assured.

As the Allies took back occupied territory, the pattern of conflict shifted away from mobile operations. Against dug-in, competent, and often fanatical Axis troops, the Allies had to apply massive firepower to winkle out resistance in a style of ground combat reminiscent of World War I. There were periods of fluid warfare, as in the African desert, or in France, Belgium, and Luxembourg after the Allies broke out from the Normandy beachheads. But in Russia, Italy, Normandy, and the Pacific, fighting was largely ditch to ditch, in a blasted landscape where misery for the individual soldier was maximized. Illustrating how we can overstate the role of armor, only 16 of 59 American divisions in Europe were armored. Of 520 German divisions in the war overall, just 40 were panzers.

With Poland eliminated and Germany reunited in the east, Hitler gathered strength to deal with the democracies in the west. Meanwhile, Russia moved to cushion its borders against Hitler: on September 17, 1939, the Soviets invaded and subsequently occupied about half of Poland. In the following months they forced Finland to relinquish some disputed territory and annexed the Baltic states of Latvia, Estonia, and Lithuania.

The United States declared its neutrality early. But President Roosevelt persuaded Congress to amend the neutrality acts that had prohibited sales of war materials to belligerents, so that France and Britain could now buy arms on a cash-and-carry basis. Crucial aid flowed from America to the democracies. Hitler attempted to cut this lifeline through submarine warfare, and the ensuing Battle of the Atlantic was pivotal in moving neutral America closer to solidarity with Europe's free nations.

In April 1940, Hitler, concerned with guaranteeing the northern flow of vital raw materials such as iron ore, struck Denmark, whose small army quickly surrendered, and Norway, which offered stiffer resistance. British and French military aid failed to save the outclassed Norwegian forces from capitulation. In May, the major blow fell in the west, but not where it was expected. The French and British, preferring the defensive, awaited a German attack. But where? On their right flank, the concrete bastions of the Maginot Line spread across northern France. The center was lightly held because it fronted the Ardennes forest, considered impassable to armor. The blow would probably fall then on the left flank, against the weak armies of neutral Holland and Belgium. Assuming this, the Allies prepared to move their main forces to support the left when Germany attacked.

But, on moving northeast into Belgium, Allied troops would enter a relatively narrow land space, where they could be trapped between attacking Axis forces and the coast. The Germans planned on it. They attacked the Allied left flank, enticing the British and French to move forward into the corridor. Panzers then swept through the Ardennes behind them, cutting them off from the body of France. Effectively, the Allies had entered a narrow room, with the door slammed behind them.

Holland surrendered quickly, and as Belgian defenses crumbled, British and French troops were forced back against the Belgian coast. But the Germans failed to capture them. The panzers paused to repair and regroup, allowing the

Allied navies, between May 26 and June 4, to rescue 224,000 British and 114,000 French soldiers from the port of Dunkirk, taking them to Britain. Bereft of outside support, the remaining French armies fought on until June 16, when they surrendered.

Hitler expected peace with Britain. But Dunkirk had changed the British mind-set. Distrustful of French commitment and reluctant to fight a second continental war, they had shown limited enthusiasm before Dunkirk. But now, backs to the wall, the British warmed to the fight. Hitler would have to invade Britain. To do this, the Luftwaffe must keep the Royal Navy from attacking his invasion fleet in the English Channel. This meant air control, which in turn necessitated destroying the modern pursuit planes of RAF Fighter Command. In the ensuing Battle of Britain, fought through the summer and autumn of 1940, the Luftwaffe failed.

British fighters were at first outnumbered, and a legend grew of the "few" who saved Britain against enormous odds. But the disparity was never that great, British fighter production passing Germany's by fall 1940. Further, Britain now had an electronic early warning system: radar. And, with key help from Polish cryptologists, Britain's Ultra intelligence unit broke the German Enigma coding system. As this transmitted operational orders, the RAF often knew the enemy's intentions, one of several key Allied intelligence triumphs in the war. The Germans had a further disadvantage. Many of their planes were designed for close ground support and had neither the range nor the performance for a strategic air offensive. Fighter bombers, like the ME110 and JU87B "Stuka," proved vulnerable to attack by the RAF's Hurricanes and Spitfires.

Failing to destroy the RAF, Germany turned to blitzing British cities to break civilian morale. But the Luftwaffe's bombers had too low a payload to achieve strategic success. In six months, they dropped only 30,000 tons on Britain, enough to enrage the victims but not crush their spirit. By comparison, in a similar period during 1944, the Allies dumped twenty times as much explosive on Germany. Unexpectedly, British morale had gone up under attack, and RAF Bomber Command was to take an enormous revenge on German cities as the war increased in ferocity.

The survival of Britain was a major factor in Germany's defeat, a watershed event, for Hitler now had an implacable enemy on his western flank, strengthened by U.S. aid. The United States, said FDR, could not be a spectator in a world dominated by force. In September 1940, America introduced a military draft, and in late autumn lend-lease was announced. Britain was running out of money, and so America would "lend" it tools of war, although the loan could not be repaid, except in favorable trade relations after the war and other concessions. America, said Roosevelt, must become "the great arsenal of democracy." The United States also extended naval protection to British-bound convoys, steadily widening the zone of American oversight to the mid-Atlantic and, by fall 1941, engaging German warships.

If Hitler's failure to crush Britain was crucial in deciding the course of the war, so was his invasion of Russia. Determined to destroy Bolshevism and gain living space to the east, Der Führer launched Operation Barbarossa on June 22, 1941. Three million Germans and their allies—Italian, Finnish, Hungarian, and Romanian soldiers—attacked in three army groups aimed at the major productive regions centered on Leningrad, Moscow, and Stalingrad. Despite huge gains in territory and captives, the massive distances frustrated Germany's bid for a knockout punch. By the onset of winter, no major city had fallen. The Soviets, whose men and equipment were better prepared for the bitter weather, counterattacked in December. Axis forces mounted offensives again in spring 1942 but could not land lethal blows. By fall they were stopped and spent the rest of the war in massively costly attempts to hold their positions.

Russia was the graveyard of the Wehrmacht (German army), which bled to death on the eastern front. By February 1942, it had lost 1,164,000 men there. The Russians paid an even higher price; without their sacrifice, the Allies could not have retaken occupied Europe. As late as D-Day, June 1944, 70 percent of Germany's manpower was on the eastern front, leaving Germany's western flank vulnerable to invasion. Barbarossa had been a huge mistake, arising from underestimation of Soviet military resilience, patriotism, and industrial capacity. Overall, the Soviets produced armor and planes superior in quality and quantity to the Axis arsenal, and they were aided after 1941 by Allied lend-lease. At one point, the Russians may have had perhaps 10,000 tanks to oppose Germany's 2,500.

The year 1942 saw a swing in the fortunes of the contending nations. It opened with renewed Axis offensives in Russia and spectacular Japanese conquests in the Far East. But it ended with the Allied nations taking back the initiative. Crucially, on December 7, 1941, the Japanese attacked the American Pacific fleet at Pearl Harbor, bringing the United States into the war—a critical factor in explaining Axis defeat. The relative fighting efficiency of Germany and Japan peaked and declined during 1942. Both had underestimated the willpower of their opponents to fight a war to the finish, despite crushing defeats; neither respected the United States, which they stereotyped as too materialistic and pleasure-loving to long endure the sacrifices of war.

Made complacent by early successes, the Axis nations cut back on aircraft and armor production as the Allies increased theirs. Although authoritarian regimes had acquired an inflated reputation for internal efficiency, they were often bungling and inefficient. The Nazi state, for example, squandered its effort by making the liquidation of "undesirables" a war aim that siphoned off resources. Though cooperation among the Allies was often faulty, it was worse between Axis nations. By May 1942, Germany knew that the Allies had cracked Japanese military codes, but it failed to alert Japan. Hitler expected significant military help from his puppet state, Vichy France, and from Franco's Spain, but it was not forthcoming. Italy was a military liability, requiring constant German bolstering.

These liabilities did not make the task of defeating the Axis easy or the best paths to victory obvious. In December 1941, at the Arcadia Conference, America and Britain established a combined military command and confronted the strategic problem of which enemy should have top priority, Germany or Japan. In the month of Pearl Harbor, with Japan making enormous gains, American public opinion favored putting the Pacific first. But American leaders agreed with the British that Hitler represented the greatest threat and could become unbeatable if he knocked Russia out of the war. Consequently, the major effort must be in Europe. The Americans pressed for an invasion of France and Germany, the heart of Hitler's Fortress Europe, in 1942 or 1943 at the latest. They felt this was necessary to help the beleaguered Russians. But the British thought this timetable too optimistic. They had tried a test landing at Dieppe on the northern coast of France in August 1942, and found Fortress Europe was a tough nut to crack, taking a high percentage of casualties.

They reasoned that a successful cross-Channel invasion would require a huge American buildup in Britain, and this in turn meant exerting every effort to win the Battle of the Atlantic. American shipping losses were heavy, partly because of inexperience with convoying techniques, and partly because the lights were not immediately turned off on the East Coast, making silhouetted merchantmen good targets for lurking U-boats. It was not until mid-1943 that the Allies won the Atlantic war, a victory due partly to growing American experience with convoying, the development of long-range bombers to protect shipping, and the equipping of escort warships with sonar, a sophisticated submarine-tracking device. And, at the end of 1942, Ultra broke the U-boat code, so the Allies could eavesdrop on undersea raiders. Of 1,175 U-boats, 785 were sunk (191 by Americans). Germany sank 23.3 million tons of Allied shipping, but the democracies built 42.5 million replacement tons. The growing Allied technological and intelligence ascendancy helps to explain their ultimate success in the war.

While the Atlantic battle continued, the British also proposed an air offensive against Germany, as well as a land attack in the Mediterranean to weaken the Axis, preliminary to an invasion of France. Why there? In pursuit of his Mediterranean empire, Mussolini had attacked Greece in October 1940. Failing badly, he sucked in the Germans, who in April–May 1941 took Greece and Crete at

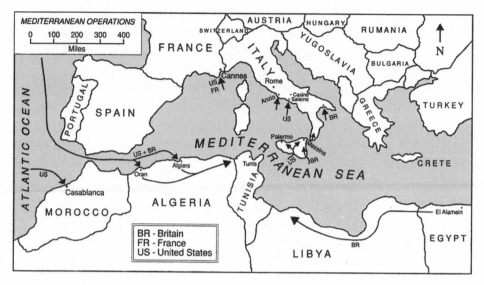

Mediterranean Operations

significant cost to their elite airborne forces. These Mediterranean air bases threatened British shipping bringing oil from the Middle East. Increasing the danger, Axis forces under General Erwin Rommel on the southern Mediterranean coast of North Africa had, by late 1942, driven through Libya to threaten Egypt and the Suez Canal. Churchill's Eighth Army faced Rommel at El Alamein. Should the British "desert rats" be defeated, the Middle East and its crucial oil fields would be lost. The British proposed landings in the German rear at Casablanca, Oran, and Algiers on the Vichy French African coast. The Americans agreed, though reluctantly, believing they were being used to salvage British imperial possessions. The campaign became Operation Torch.

In October 1942, the Eighth Army attacked and, in November, British-American forces under General Dwight D. Eisenhower's overall command landed on the Vichy coast behind Rommel. This successful amphibious landing against a relatively weak opponent gave the Allies invaluable experience, though at a cost. Allied intelligence failed to properly utilize sympathetic French officers prepared to cooperate rather than fight. Some untried Allied equipment proved a liability, such as the American Grant tank, with a cannon traverse of only 180 degrees, covering just half the battlefield. GIs wearing sunglasses were killed by snipers, who caught sunlight glinting off lenses. Some British armor was squandered in piecemeal frontal attacks. Still, the Axis forces, outnumbered, bereft of air support, taken in front and rear, were trapped in a pocket on the Tunisian coast, surrendering on May 10, 1943.

Having secured Africa and the Middle East, the Allies moved north, attacking Sicily to seize a foothold in the northern Mediterranean. Britain's Eighth Army was to make the main thrust up Sicily's eastern coast, targeting the port of Messina, the Axis garrison's escape route to the Italian mainland. Patton's American Seventh Army would shield their left flank. Allied forces landed successfully on July 10, 1943, although naval gunners shot down some of their own airborne troops and others drowned in the sea. The British met stiff German resistance, but Patton knifed through weak Italian opposition on the west coast of the island before turning east to race for Messina. He was slowed by a determined German rearguard action, and, the Allies failing to seal the pocket, 40,000 Axis soldiers slipped off the island before Messina fell on August 17.

The debate over strategic aims now continued. Churchill strenuously championed an invasion of Italy, to force its surrender and make Hitler transfer troops from France to fill the void. This shift of German resources would make a cross-Channel invasion easier. Also, with Italian bases, Allied bombers could reach industrial targets in Germany and the Balkans. The plan had the disadvantage of diluting the Allied troop buildup for an early invasion of France, which the Americans wanted. They argued an Italian invasion would prove an indecisive diversion. Churchill and FDR reached a compromise by which there would be an attack on Italy, but the resources allotted to that front would be small enough not to jeopardize the invasion of France. This solution made diplomatic sense, although the two-front war arguably meant that Allied forces in the Italian theater were too weak to prevent a stalemate. Allied troops in Italy believed they were sacrificed by political leaders.

Allied forces landed in Italy on September 8 and 9, 1943, provoking Italy's surrender. The Germans rushed troops into Italy. Taking advantage of the rugged terrain, neutralizing the Allied advantage in armor and providing strong natural defensive positions, the Wehrmacht contested every hill and valley in a physically and mentally grueling ground war. An attempt to outflank the Germans by landing at Anzio in their rear, on January 22, 1944, was contained by panzers, and though Rome fell on June 4, 1944, it was not until May 2, 1945, that German troops in Italy finally surrendered.

The Germans' defense in depth elicited a massive heavy-weapons response, pounding first Sicily and then Italy's infrastructure. Les Gerencer, a GI who saw the ruins of Caltanissetta, Sicily, July 18, 1943, recalled, "All you could smell was the dead in the rubble, and the people on the side looking at you like you was some kinda bug" (Garland, 69–70). Although glad to be rid of the Nazis, many European civilians deeply resented the brute force nature of the Allied advance. In another incident, Allied bombers ruined the ancient monastery of Monte Cassino with its priceless medieval library, the operations officers believing incorrectly that Germans were dug in there. Illustrating that this was a total war in which no one was safe in a war zone, the destruction disrupted agriculture and industry, destroyed homes, and threw much of the population into starvation, beggary, and prostitution.

While the Mediterranean campaigns were progressing, American and British air forces attacked targets in occupied Europe and Germany. Their aims were threefold: to diminish industrial production, particularly of oil and machine parts; to soften up Fortress Europe for the cross-Channel invasion; and to assure the Soviets that the democracies were pulling their weight. In August 1942,

The Abbey of Monte Cassino. Painting by Tom Craig.
Courtesy of the U.S. Army Center of Military History

the American Eighth Air Force began flying bombing missions from British bases and, in late 1943, Twelfth Air Force bombers from Italian fields attacked targets in Germany and the Balkans. Yet the U.S. air buildup took time. In autumn 1943, American bomb tonnage represented only 15 percent of the theater total, and it did not reach parity with the RAF until February 1944.

In mid-1941, the British abandoned the illusion that they could hit military-industrial targets with surgical accuracy. RAF bombsights were so imprecise that only 25 percent of bombs fell within five miles of the objective. Also, precision bombing could be attempted only in daylight, with huge losses of bombers to air defenses. So, the RAF went to nighttime "area bombing" of industrial districts, hoping to create widespread damage and civilian demoralization. This began a deliberate policy of carpet bombing that remains controversial today.

Americans, disturbed by the collateral damage done to civilian areas by the night raids, stuck to daylight bombing. They hoped the B-17 Flying Fortress and B-24 Liberator had the firepower and speed to defend themselves in daylight while delivering bomb loads accurately with the Norden bombsight. Initially, these daylight raids proved costly. In July 1943, 100 planes and 1,000 crewmen were lost. A further 75 airmen had mental breakdowns. In the October 14 raid on the Schweinfurt ball bearing factories, 60 of 291 Fortresses were lost. Conditions improved with the introduction, in December 1943, of the P-51 Mustang, a long-range fighter capable of providing to-the-target protection. But losses remained high. In the February 2–26, 1944, raids on aircraft factories, the American Air Force lost 226 bombers, 28 fighters, and 2,600 men.

Accurate bombing remained elusive: under perfect conditions, only 50 percent of American bombs fell within a quarter mile of the target. Fighter attack, flak, smoke, and cloud cover lowered efficiency. American flyers estimated that as many as 90 percent of bombs might miss the target. For example, raids on the submarine pens at Saint-Nazaire and Lorient destroyed adjacent French towns but left the targets undamaged. The high costs to civilians, not only in Germany but also in the occupied countries, created widespread resentment of the Allies.

How do we judge the strategic air offensive against Fortress Europe? On the one hand, hopes that air power offered a unilaterally economical, clinical, and humane method of winning victory outright proved illusory. The official U.S. *Strategic Bombing Survey* (1946) estimated that a million dollars in planes, bases, crews, and bombs were spent to do a million dollars in damage. And you still needed boots on the ground to force enemy surrender. Air attacks extended the human costs of war. At least 635,000 German civilian men, women, and children died, along with thousands more in the occupied countries.

On the other hand, not all civilian losses were outside the perimeters of acceptable conduct. In modern war, the distinction between military and civilian targets becomes blurred. When bombers attacked a factory, a railroad marshaling yard, a dock, an oil refinery, or an electrical power system, they inevitably killed workers and their families. But these civilians were part of the war effort. Was it legitimate to kill soldiers with rifles but not those who made their weapons? It is true that rage against the enemy, called "war psychosis," grew as the war extended indefinitely, producing a mutual, escalating ferocity. This resulted in some Allied air attacks going beyond legitimate targeting of military sites and causing needless destruction. But recent scholarship has modified downward earlier estimates of the extent of such gratuitous brutality.

A notorious case is Dresden, which was attacked on February 13 and 14, 1945, by the RAF and U.S. Air Force, creating a firestorm in the city center. However, Dresden was not, as some critics claimed, an open, undefended city with neither industrial nor military significance. It housed important light engineering and was a strategic rail hub for the movement of enemy forces. The claim that up to 135,000 people were killed has been reliably recalculated down to between 25 and 40,000. This remains a large number and not an attractive picture. Yet the air offensive, of which Dresden was a part, made significant contributions to Allied victory in western Europe.

Although German industrial production climbed, the rate would have been higher without the bombings. Air attacks on Axis fuel production, begun in March 1944, impeded enemy mobility in the air and on the ground. And historians now suspect that, although the German blitz of British urban centers raised the victims' morale, the utter annihilation of German cities crushed much of the will to fight on. Also, by deliberately using their bombers as decoys in daylight raids and accepting a high cost in crews, the American high command drew the Luftwaffe into a battle of attrition that virtually destroyed it by D-Day, giving Allied ground forces complete air cover. From March to September 1944, Allied fighter bombers targeted transportation networks in the invasion area, effectively preventing German armored reserves from entering the battle.

Controversy surrounds the Allies' decision not to bomb open the concentration camps, freeing the inmates. This was logistically possible by early 1944 and, by late in that year, Allied planes were literally starved of targets of opportunity, the enemy infrastructure having been fatally downgraded. But the question was not a simple one. Air attacks would undoubtedly have killed many inmates. Denis Avey, a British flyer in Auschwitz when U.S. planes raided nearby industrial facilities in August 1944, said that errant bombs hitting the camps created massive damage and attendant casualties. Moreover, the Allies feared that large numbers of displaced persons wandering the countryside in wake of a break-out would seriously impede Allied ground operations. It seemed better to concentrate resources on defeating the enemy in the field.

* * *

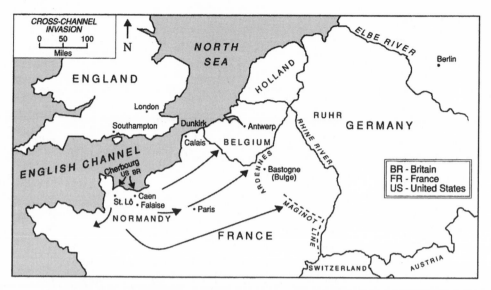

The Cross-Channel Invasion

By 1944, the European Axis was fatally weakened. Italy had surrendered and, in the east, the Soviets made huge advances. By October, Finland, Romania, Bulgaria, and Hungary were out of the war. Yet the conflict could not be ended without a frontal attack on the western face of Hitler's Fortress Europe: France. The D-Day invasion, begun June 6, 1944, was the largest cooperative amphibious operation in history, involving troops from America, Britain and its Commonwealth, the Free French, and other European exiles. The offensive secured for the Western Allies a vital beachhead in Normandy. On Day One, after a massive air and naval bombardment, Allied paratroops neutralized key coastal locations, despite some confusion in the air and heavy losses on the ground. In the follow-up, waves of 176,000 men in 4,000 landing craft assaulted the beaches.

Allied intelligence was crucial to success in the Normandy invasion, tricking Hitler into believing that the major landing would come further north, at Calais. By now, the British had turned every German spy in the United Kingdom, so that their carefully concocted false reports home helped to perpetrate the hoax. A phantom American army group under General George Patton was created, existing mainly on paper, and seemingly poised to attack the target anticipated by Hitler. Awaiting this offensive, the German leader held back crucial armored reserves, which, when they finally moved, lost heavily to Allied fighter bombers.

By the end of June, a million Allied troops were ashore, along with 177,000 vehicles and 586,000 tons of supplies. When Cherbourg fell, the invaders had a deep-water port to replace their temporary artificial harbors, assuring their ability to sustain the beachhead. The Germans still proved stubborn opponents. At Omaha Beach, veteran panzers nearly succeeded in denying Americans the beachhead. The landing was also handicapped by the Americans' failure to realize the need for specialized equipment to sweep the shore of obstacles like underwater mines. The Wehrmacht, though bereft of air cover and armor, made excellent defensive positions out of the thick Normandy hedgerows made of earth, stone, and trees. The Allies tried to smash through them with bombs and shells. But the obstacles finally had to be punctured by bulldozers fitted with improvised plough blades.

Allied tanks did not have the firepower needed to spearhead a breakthrough without massive artillery or air support fire. The infantry, too, called for a deluge of shells or bombs to clear the path ahead and save friendly lives. "We let the artillery fight the war as much as possible," said one U.S. infantry officer (Ellis, 384). The result was massive destruction to the environment on a wide front. Ironically, the devastation hindered Allied progress. Cherbourg was so battered it took three weeks to clear it for traffic. Caen, the first major British objective, was pounded into rubble, blocking the roads armored vehicles needed to advance.

Finally, on July 25, the American First Army, under Omar Bradley, broke out of the pocket at Saint-Lo and reintroduced mobility to the battlefront. Part of the Third Army, led by George Patton, back again in field command, exploited the gap, swinging west to try to free the ports of Brittany. The remaining U.S. forces wheeled east to drive across France. The pace was so fast that a large part of the German Seventh Army was in danger of being outflanked and trapped between the Americans and the British and Canadians, advancing to the north. The Germans were able to hold open an escape route at Falaise long enough for 35,000 men to escape entrapment. They were helped by inadequate British-American coordination. But 10,000 Germans were killed, and 30,000 surrendered.

Meanwhile, a further U.S. and Free French landing in southern France strengthened Allied momentum and led to the fall of Marseilles, a port whose facilities greatly aided military supply. Paris was liberated on August 25, and the swift American advance continued into northern France. By mid-September, the Germans were largely out of France and Belgium. At the same time, the British advanced on the left toward Holland, targeting Antwerp. Further ports were needed to keep the armies supplied with fuel, as shortages began to seriously slow progress. Antwerp was a logical choice. British Field Marshal Bernard Montgomery took the city in early September. However, he failed to dislodge German artillery emplaced along the banks of the estuary from the sea to the city, so that shipping access was hindered until November 29.

Montgomery's attention was distracted from Antwerp because, for some time, he had been urging a daring plan upon Eisenhower. The speed of Allied mechanized advance was outrunning gas supply. Montgomery requested the bulk of the remaining fuel for a drive that might collapse German resistance before the end of the year. He proposed a bold thrust through the Netherlands that would flank Germany's West Wall defenses and surge into the northern regions of the Reich. The plan was imaginative but too ambitious: it relied on special forces taking and holding four rivers and three canals to open a path for Allied armor. The high command ignored Ultra's warning that panzer strength in the area was greater than anticipated. The upshot was that Operation Market Garden failed, and as winter approached, the Allied offensives, bereft of fuel, ground to a halt opposite Germany's Siegfried line of defenses.

Hitler now launched his last major offensive in the west. He hoped to repeat the success of 1940, by again attacking in the Ardennes and driving through weak American forces in what was still designated by Allied generals (incredibly, given the experience of 1940) a quiet sector. We must remember this and other significant Allied intelligence failures when assessing the overall role of intelligence in the war. After the breakthrough, German armor would then race to the coast at Antwerp, dividing the Allied armies and defeating them piecemeal.

On December 16, 1944, twenty-five German divisions attacked, taking advantage of bad weather that kept Allied planes grounded. In hard fighting, they dented the American line, and, in a further intelligence success, Germans dressed as Americans sowed confusion and demoralization behind enemy lines. But, although they bent the American front, the Germans could not pierce it, creating only a "bulge." They had achieved complete tactical surprise, but they simply did not have the strength for a major breakthrough. Unlike 1940, the Germans did not face weak, outmoded opponents. Some of the forces Hitler insisted were available for a spectacular putsch existed only in his mind, now degenerating.

When the weather cleared, Allied air power blunted the German advance. American ground forces struck back, including elements of Patton's Third Army which, in a remarkable feat, wheeled out of line and drove hard from the east to help beat back the German advance in the Bastogne area. The Battle of the Bulge spent the Wehrmacht's last strength, and Germany lay open to assault. The western Allies crossed the Rhine on March 1, 1945, and met the Russians at the Elbe on April 25, as they poured in from the east. On April 30, Hitler committed suicide and nazism collapsed with him.

Germany, along with much of continental Europe, lay in ruins; this was the havoc that Hitler had wrought. Believing that in World War I Germany had surrendered while there was still a good chance of victory, he preferred total destruction to the repetition of failure. Thus, a war of brute force destruction was made inevitable, in which Germany's resistance went beyond any logical defense of state interests and provoked national destruction. In the Wehrmacht, the Allies had faced an opponent too skilled to be beaten with the same ease displayed by the panzers in 1939 and 1940. In both east and west, the Axis armies had to be hammered into destruction. A conflict fought to unconditional surrender had brought about such intense mayhem that war psychosis was provoked on both sides. In the ruins of European cities, we learned of our ability as a species to wreak havoc on each other and our environment in proportions hitherto unimagined.

In the Pacific, as in Europe, the pattern of war was marked in its early stages by lightning offensives. Japan's conquests reflected bold planning and execution. In three months, imperial forces overran territory half the size of the United States. On December 7, 1941, Japanese carrier-based planes attacked the American Pacific fleet at Pearl Harbor, sinking four battleships and three destroyers, as well as severely damaging numerous other vessels. They also destroyed 160 aircraft and disabled 128 others, with a loss of only 29 Japanese planes.

Simultaneously, Japanese forces struck at Western bases in the Philippines, Thailand, Malaya, Wake Island, Guam, and Hong Kong. In February 1942, the British bastion of Singapore fell too easily to an unanticipated land assault. The Netherlands Indies capitulated in March, followed by Burma in April. The Japanese also seized strong positions in New Guinea and the Solomons. Only in the Philippines, where U.S. and Filipino troops clung to the Bataan peninsula and Corregidor, was the conquest slowed. However, by May 6, 1942, these Allied outposts had also fallen. The Japanese were on the doorstep of Australia and needed only to take the Hawaiian islands to exclude the United States from the Pacific.

Several factors aided Japan's lightning war, including Western arrogance. Used to easily crushing poorly equipped and trained Asian armies, the West did not believe until too late what their intelligence reports told them about superior Japanese military strength and efficiency. The command at Pearl Harbor dismissed warnings of impending attack (leading later conspiracy theorists to charge, incorrectly, that President Roosevelt deliberately invited attack to force America through the back door into war). This was not treason but complacency. Even after the war began, General Douglas MacArthur in the Philippines failed to disperse his aircraft properly. Over half the modern bombers and fighters in the theater were still parked in neat rows, providing a shooting gallery when the Japanese hit Clark Field. MacArthur had not conceived of this possibility.

Much to the Western military planners' surprise, they were outclassed technologically in the opening rounds of the conflict. The Japanese Zero fighter outranked any Allied plane in the theater, such as the Brewster Buffalo. And, in 1941, Japanese pilots were among the best-trained anywhere. The two weapons assumed capable of negating a Japanese invasion of the Philippines did not work: American submarines were handicapped by inferior torpedoes, and the B-17 bomber proved ineffective against naval targets. Japanese armies also

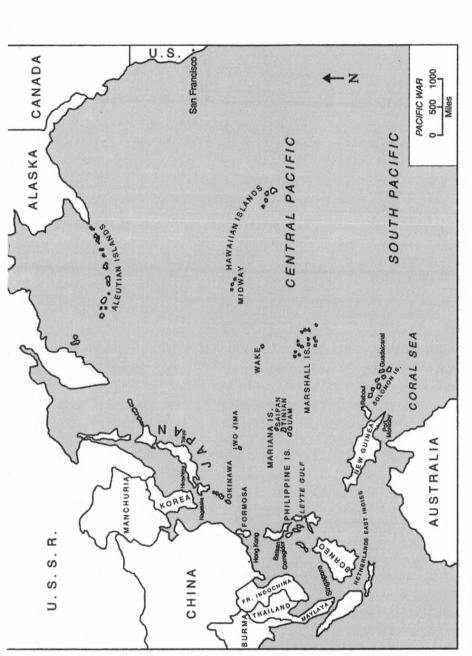

The Pacific War

surprised their opponents by their logistical successes: they moved faster and further than the Western Allies believed possible, negotiating terrain their opponents thought impassable.

Western armies, highly bureaucratized and heavily dependent on lines of communication for their many material needs, required anywhere from eight to twenty-eight service personnel to keep one man on the firing line. In the Japanese army, the ratio was more like one to one. Why? Each man subsisted lightly on a basic diet of rice, a little dried fish or meat serving merely as a supplement. Also, the imperial Institute of Tropical Warfare had studied edible wild plants in the war zones, adding vitamin-high vegetation to the diet. Put succinctly, the Japanese military animal dragged a lot less tail than the Allied armies, so they covered ground quickly.

The Japanese were also helped initially by an ironic reversal in Western attitudes. Never characterized as simply human by their enemies, the Japanese went from being scorned as subhuman before December 1941 to being feared as superhuman immediately after. One reason that Allied bastions fell so easily early in the war was that command confidence and troop morale crumbled in face of lightning Japanese offensives. In 1942, British Commonwealth and U.S. troops collapsed before relatively small Japanese forces, which had acquired an almost supernatural status. To combat this, Allied propaganda tried to deflate the image of Japanese soldiers by depicting them as degenerate—a species of nasty little monkeys or, worse, vile insects, grubs and ants to be exterminated.

Why, then, after such spectacular opening victories, did Japan's war effort fail? To begin with, Japan, unlike the United States and its allies, never saw the war as one for total conquest and domination of its major opponents. Contrary to belief at the time, no Japanese leader seriously considered invading the United States. Japan fought for recognition, a place in the sun alongside Westerners. The best Japanese military minds, such as Admiral Isoroku Yamamoto, knew that in a war of attrition Japan must lose. Their hope was to initially seize such a vast area of the Pacific that the price of taking it back would be too daunting and Westerners would reach a compromise peace, acknowledging Japan's right to a sphere of influence in the region. (At their furthest extent, Japanese conquests ran from the Aleutians and the tip of Alaska in the north to New Guinea at Australia's border in the south.) Japan's aim was the sharing of power.

Racially stereotyping their opponents as coarse barbarians not imbued with the finer military spirit, the Japanese underrated their enemies' staying power and determination. They failed to grasp the absolute resentment their attack would generate in their enemies: the Japanese offensive was seen by its victims as a war of choice, not a defensive war of necessity. In response, unconditional surrender, the eradication of Japanese militarism, would dominate Allied thinking up through the dropping of the atomic bombs.

In a protracted war, Japan had some hope of holding out by drawing from the resources of the conquered regions to refurbish its war machine. But the Allies rebounded too quickly for this possibility to be made good, taking back territory and choking off Japan's maritime trade routes. Also, through racial arrogance and gratuitous cruelty, the Japanese military alienated other Asian peoples who might have worked with them. Japan was forced to fight a war to the death on chronically inadequate, dwindling resources. As the tide changed, the weaknesses in imperial military thinking became apparent. Japan in the 1930s had tied itself to the albatross of an endless China war. This was a major factor in ultimate Japanese defeat, a disproportionate percentage of the imperial army being tied down in the Chinese theater. Allied assistance to Generalissimo Chiang Kai-shek, together with the opening of subsidiary fronts in Burma and on the borders of India, helped to sap Japan's land-based fighting strength.

Japan's naval technology and fighting methods, innovative in the beginning stages of the war, quickly lagged behind the Allies. Japan lost naval air battles because its ships and planes did not have radar, a basic tool for locating the enemy. Despite embarking on maritime conquest, the navy neglected vital elements of domination in modern sea warfare. Some senior officers continued to see the battleship as the heart of the fleet, even after their own bombers had shown the vulnerability of capital ships to air attack. For example, due to the dominant experience of flying ground support missions off the China coast, aircraft carriers were seen primarily as floating platforms from which to attack land targets rather than as vital weapons in the war at sea. The result was fatal errors, such as at Midway, where Japanese carrier planes attacked the island defenses of Midway first, instead of seeking out the enemy's aircraft carriers. Consequently, American naval flyers were able to catch the Japanese refueling on deck and smashed their carrier force.

Japan did not build sufficient submarines to interdict the Allied invasion fleets that took back imperial conquests. Acting on an antiquated sense of honor, for much of the war the Japanese high command would not allow submarines to sink merchant vessels; only warships were seen as fair game. Hence, Japan failed to cut the supply lines that fed and armed the enemy forces closing in on the home islands. Submarines were also frittered away in futile attempts to supply Japanese garrisons on beleaguered Pacific islands, the boats carrying too little cargo capacity to carry out the mission effectively.

Japan's survival depended on merchantmen taking supplies to its troops on the Pacific perimeter and bringing back raw materials to turn into weapons of war. A merchant marine that was the third largest in the world in 1941 was decimated by Allied air and underwater attacks. Adequate convoying techniques were not developed, and the Japanese were blind to the crucial role of radio technology

in antisubmarine warfare. Most Japanese vessels had no listening devices to locate boats underwater. Partly, the problem came from lack of resources and
tools to build new machinery, but partly, too, it reflected a continuing struggle
between conservatives and innovators in the Japanese navy. Officers of the old
school, steeped in traditions modeled on the British Royal Navy of World War
I, were often resistant to change.

From mid-1942 onward, the conclusion of the Pacific war was not in doubt.
Even the apparent Japanese coup at Pearl Harbor contained an omen of disaster, for the crucial weapons of Pacific naval war, three U.S. carriers, were away
from the harbor. The Japanese, concentrating on the battleships and land-based
aircraft, got none of them. The United States retained sufficient naval power to
end Japan's seaborne invasions in two pivotal battles. The Allies were also helped
by Magic, the name for another intelligence achievement, the deciphering of Japan's diplomatic codes that gave vital advance warning of enemy intentions. On
May 7–8, 1942, in the Battle of the Coral Sea, Allied naval and land forces turned
back a Japanese amphibious group bound for Port Moresby in southern New
Guinea, opposite the Australian coast. Japan's southward thrust was terminated.
A month later, during June 3–6, Japanese forces steaming toward Hawaii were
precisely identified by Allied intelligence and "ambushed" in a crushing defeat
at Midway, ending their expansion in the central Pacific.

With Japan's Pacific initiatives ended, the Allies struck back. The first targets
were Japanese garrisons in New Guinea and the Solomon islands to the east, positions from which aircraft could interdict Allied communication with Australia. During summer, 1942, American and British Commonwealth forces drove
back the Japanese in New Guinea. In August, American forces assaulted three
of the Solomon islands: Gavutu, Tulagi, and Guadalcanal. Savage fighting on
the latter did not end until February 1943, but the Japanese army had suffered
its first major defeat of modern times. Combined with the Coral Sea and Midway, these actions turned the war around.

Some who fought in the Pacific, including General MacArthur, believed that
this theater was neglected because of FDR's promise to Churchill to put Europe
first. In fact, the administration devoted serious attention to the Pacific, which
it saw as a special American sphere of interest—so that there was actually a huge
buildup of American strength in the Pacific. In December 1943, there were more
American troops and equipment in the Pacific than in Europe. By 1944 the U.S.
Navy had three times Japan's 1941 strength. In the struggle for Okinawa, fought
April to June 1945, and typical of late-war Pacific battles, a starving Japanese garrison of 120,000 faced 250,000 Americans armed with enormous firepower.

The plethora of American resources allowed for a two-pronged strategy in the
Pacific. From Australia in the south, MacArthur, army commander in the the-

ater, pushed northwest, severing Japan's transportation network with the resource-rich Netherlands Indies. He then retook the Philippines, restoring America's bruised martial pride and providing bases for a bomber offensive against Japan. Meanwhile, a navy and marine offensive, under Admiral Chester Nimitz, used Hawaii as a staging post to push westward across the central Pacific. Nimitz had two major objectives: the Marianas, linchpin of Japan's supply system in the central Pacific, and the Formosa-China coast, from which bombers could also be launched against the Japanese home islands.

This two-pronged offensive strategy has been criticized as a needless duplication of effort that cost lives and resources best used in other ways. The failure to choose between the two invasion routes perhaps reflected a political desire to avoid interservice rivalry between the army and the navy, rather than advancing a legitimate military agenda. On the one hand, it can be argued that the central Pacific route was the more direct and that MacArthur's thrust against the well-defended Philippines should have been avoided. On the other hand, it can be said that for Filipino and American morale, the return of MacArthur was indispensable and the navy would have been better employed in total effort against Japanese commerce rather than in island-taking. In the end, both arguments may be colored by hindsight. At the time, the Japanese empire seemed so strong and its military so effective that assaults from two directions to pin down their resources appeared sensible.

Savage early fighting provoked the policy of "island hopping." The Japanese expected that they could wear down the Allied will to fight by exacting a huge toll for each island retaken. For example, they assumed MacArthur must assault Raboul, a bastion of 100,000 Japanese on the northern tip of New Britain Island, seemingly blocking his advance. But Raboul, bereft of offensive capability by sea or air, could be safely bypassed, leaving the impotent garrison to starve.

This maneuver set a pattern for much of the Pacific war. By October 1944, MacArthur had leapfrogged his way north into the Philippines. Here he fought the decisive Battle of Leyte Gulf, which smashed Japanese resistance in his area. It has been said that MacArthur chose a strategy of bypass to avoid the slaughter he had witnessed in World War I static ground fighting, and that Nimitz, without this land-based experience, committed his forces to more costly frontal assaults. Yet, MacArthur, too, has been faulted for turning to costly mopping-up operations, unnecessarily spending lives and damaging the environment.

In mid-June 1944, Nimitz's forces struck the Marianas, capturing Tinian, Guam, and Saipan, 1,350 miles from Japan's capital. The ring was closing. By February 1945, marines were fighting for Iwo Jima, only 750 miles from Tokyo. The Japanese fought back with desperate bravery and increasing effectiveness. At Saipan and earlier, the imperial army tried to contest the initial landings, only to be devastated by enormous American firepower targeting the open beaches. After Saipan, the defenders waited inland in prepared positions, difficult to locate and eradicate. They fought with desperate intensity, often attacking in mass suicide assaults: given the ferocity that by now characterized both sides, many saw no point in trying to surrender. The result was seen at Iwo Jima: to win its eight square miles of land, the marines took 27,000 casualties. On Okinawa, attacked April 1, the United States sustained 48,000 casualties, while nearly all 120,000 defenders died.

Deepening mutual terror and horror, kamikazes attacked warships supporting the landings. Due to successful Allied attacks on Japan's industries and shipping lanes, competitive fighter aircraft could no longer be produced. Nor was there enough fuel to fully train pilots. Therefore, barely trained adolescents were sent to ram enemy ships with crude planes, equipped with no navigational aids but crammed with explosives. Fighters and antiaircraft fire stopped most kamikazes getting through, but their ineffectiveness was not as influential as the image they left of irrational fanaticism. Furthering this impression, in April 1945, the battleship *Yamato* was ordered to attack the American fleet. With no air cover or support vessels, the doomed ship was sunk with huge loss of life. The ferocity of Japanese resistance colored Allied estimates of the likely high cost of forcing final victory and ways of avoiding this.

Like Germany, Japan was subjected to intense bomber attacks. Starting in June 1944, new B-29 Superfortresses, with the highest bomb load of any Allied plane, began hitting industrial targets. In early 1945, General Curtis Le May, heading the Twenty-first Bomber Command, initiated the incendiary bombing of cities, whose residential districts of wood and paper houses were especially vulnerable to fire. On March 9, three hundred B-29s hit Tokyo with napalm, creating an inferno of 1,800° Fahrenheit. Sixteen square miles of the city and 85,000 people were incinerated. Fire raids followed on Nagoya, Osaka, Kobe, Yokohama, and other cities, with similarly devastating results. In all, sixty-one cities were bombed, destroying 40 percent of their surface area and causing about 672,000 casualties.

Given stupendous Japanese losses, why did the government not surrender? Some leaders, particularly in the military, still felt the home islands could be defended. And the warrior code of Bushido dictated a sacrifice beyond the rational interests of state or people. Also, the growing peace party lacked effective leadership, especially as the emperor, though increasingly convinced of the need for peace, took a largely passive role. The peace cause was handicapped by the Allied demand for unconditional surrender, promulgated at the 1943 Casablanca Conference. Japanese leaders feared this meant removing the emperor, who enjoyed a quasi-religious status in Japanese culture, epitomizing the nation's soul. His survival could be key to retaining political and psychological stability

Louseous Japanicas

The first serious outbreak of this lice epidemic was officially noted on December 7, 1941, at Honolulu, T. H. To the Marine Corps, especially trained in combating this type of pestilence, was assigned the gigantic task of extermination. Extensive experiments on Guadalcanal, Tarawa, and Saipan have shown that this louse inhabits coral atolls in the South Pacific, particularly pill boxes, palm trees, caves, swamps and jungles.

Flame throwers, mortars, grenades and bayonets have proven to be an effective remedy. But before a complete cure may be effected the origin of the plague, the breeding grounds around the Tokyo area, must be completely annihilated.

The Japanese as a louse to be exterminated.
Leatherneck Magazine, March 1945. Courtesy of the Marine Corps Association

in the stricken nation. The government did put out tentative peace feelers through a third party, the Soviet Union, not yet a belligerent in the Pacific. The Western powers knew about this through Magic intelligence intercepts, but they doubted the seriousness of Japan's intentions and worried that a positive response might be interpreted as indecisiveness, encouraging Japanese fanatics.

In this atmosphere of stalemate and mounting destruction, President Harry Truman (FDR had died on April 12) decided to drop the two existing atomic bombs on Japanese cities. Hiroshima was attacked on August 6 and Nagasaki on August 9, killing roughly 135,000 people and forcing Japan's surrender. The military arguments surrounding the bombings are complex, but pivotal is whether Japan would have surrendered without their use or the alternative, an invasion of the home islands (scheduled to begin in November). Intelligence estimates suggested conventional assault might cost a million Allied casualties and enormous devastation to Japan. Some military men argued that Japan could collapse without an invasion, attacks on shipping and industry having devastated the country's defensive capacity. A blockade would suffice to strangle resistance. Others disagreed, and, even if an invasion were avoided, more Allied lives would be lost in the weeks of bombing and sea warfare that remained. In the emotional climate of 1945, an environment of destruction and escalating hatred, Allied leaders cannot be expected to have considered sacrificing Allied servicemen to save Japanese civilians. Moreover, as reserving the atomic bombs would have meant continued incendiary attacks, concern over civilian lives seemed moot.

Could the bomb have been demonstrated without destroying a city? Some scientists who worked on the weapons wanted this. The risk was that, if the test bomb failed to work properly, its impact would be squandered. Then, as the Allies had only two, the second would have to be dropped on a city and, if it failed to provoke surrender, no follow-up remained. So a demonstration was ruled out. What is more questionable is that only three days were allowed to elapse between the two atomic attacks. Two days after Hiroshima, Russia declared war on Japan, sealing its fate. The peace party was gaining ground, particularly as most senior army officers now accepted the inevitability of defeat. Little would have been lost to the Allies by waiting a further few days and perhaps guaranteeing the position of the emperor. Ironically, the emperor was allowed to remain— after Nagasaki and the Japanese surrender.

But we must also remember the context. The long-term effects of radiation were not understood. Humanity had been forced to witness enormous destruction all through World War II. By 1945, the killing had reached such gigantic proportions that the bombing of two more cities did not invoke the moral qualms that emerged later. *Time* magazine, for example, had advocated the systematic obliteration of thirty-one German cities to shorten the ground war. In such a time of death, the unimaginable had become the acceptable. The truth is that it was politically impossible for Truman not to use the bombs. The American public was war weary and wanted the troops home. The president could not refuse to use all the weapons in his arsenal to bring a swift resolution; we had them, and so we used them.

In the Pacific, Japan's grim defense of the islands necessitated the same brute force patterns of warfare that Hitler's refusal to yield ground produced in Europe. We had plenty of ammunition and used it to save friendly lives; perhaps 1,500 artillery rounds were fired to kill each Japanese soldier. In the final fight with the battleship *Yamato*, planes from one American carrier alone fired 1.5 million rounds of small-caliber ammunition from their machine guns. Japanese suicidal fanaticism had produced a corresponding insensitivity to killing on the part of Allied soldiers, who butchered their opponents in staggering quantities—over 100,000 on Okinawa, alone. The ecology of some islands was so badly damaged that it had not recovered twenty years later. And humanity had been introduced to the nuclear age, from which there was no going back.

CHAPTER THREE

The American War Machine

The American war machine that came into full being after Pearl Harbor was colossal. It is doubtful that the Allies could have won without America's participation. With America in the war, it is equally doubtful that they could have lost. This scenario, however, was not inevitable. In the 1930s, many Americans were alienated from Europe's problems by disillusion over the unsatisfactory results of World War I. This feeling helped to produce isolationism and the America First campaign. Axis leaders misread American skepticism as weakness, a fatal softness bred of consumerism. Americans would not wage effective war, said Hermann Göring, head of Germany's Luftwaffe; their forte was producing razor blades, not artillery.

Some Americans had feared he was right. Yet, in December 1941, the nation came alive, like a giant awaking from sleep, people said. American industry provided the needs of its own military and contributed substantially to arming its allies. The United States was the only nation able to field and fully equip major armies in both western Europe and Asia. Inevitably, because of its sheer size and importance, America's contribution came to be overstated in our popular culture; the U.S. war machine morphed from a primary factor in Axis defeat to the only factor. Oliver L. North, a marine veteran and social commentator of the next generation, wrote in 1991 that World War II was "the war that America won for the world" (North and Novak, 64).

A legend of superlatives grew around the war effort: the United States outproduced everyone else, and American machines were the best on the planet.

"When Hitler put his war on wheels he ran it straight down our alley," asserted General Brehon B. Somervell in 1942. There was a new champion on the battlefield, he said, and "it's called Detroit" (Keegan and Holmes, 236). In the popular view, America's soldiers outclassed all others; they were savvy fighters, deeply committed, superbly led, superior in morale and morals. We think the draft was completely fair, and the military functioned like a well-knit family. So, we say, did the nation: the cause was not marred by racial or gender tensions. Harmony characterized the home front. Men went to war while women took to the production line. Surely, everyone put a hand to the wheel, and Rosie the Riveter symbolized a can-do country. In imagination, it was the best of wars.

The reality was more complex. Manufacture of war materials was vital to victory, but there were problems in the industrial sector. Many GIs were not happy warriors. The draft and military culture functioned well to create huge citizen armies, but ethnic, gender, and class tensions were inevitable. It is untrue that every man fought and each woman worked. Of 16 million military personnel, 25 percent never left the United States, and less than 50 percent of those overseas entered a battle zone. Only 8 percent of wives had husbands in the military; a majority of married men were civilians working at home. Most women remained housewives; of 33 million women at home in December 1941, seven out of eight were still there in 1944, at the peak of wartime employment. Nine out of ten young mothers did not work outside the home.

Of working women, only 16 percent were in war industries, partly because men did not want their wives in the grimy, often dangerous, war plants where, due to round-the-clock production, they were also open to sexual advances on the night shift. A 1943 Gallup poll showed that 70 percent of married men opposed war work for their wives and that 75 percent of spouses agreed. GI surveys showed that the soldiers' dream was not Rosie the Riveter but *Mrs. Miniver* (1942), Hollywood's model housewife (played by Greer Garson), who kept familiar and respectable family values alive during shifting times. Many middle-class women felt blue-collar work was demeaning. And some wives worried that if they became self-supporting, their husbands were more likely to be drafted.

To get a realistic picture of the U.S. war machine, let us begin with its industrial arm. For most of the 1930s, congressional military appropriations were minimal, averaging $180 million annually. On September 1, 1939, when Hitler invaded Poland, the army could fully equip only 75,000 of its 227,000 personnel. Even when government began to prepare for war, some businesses refused to cooperate. Automakers, still recovering from the depression, feared abandoning domestic-market profits—in 1941, Detroit turned out a million more cars than in 1939—to produce military vehicles. Even after Pearl Harbor, Standard Oil insisted on honoring its chemical contracts with I. G. Farben, a synthetic rubber manufacturer for Hitler's military, so that for nine months of the war the Axis received American aid.

Still, after painful initial adjustments, American production lines during the war effort turned out approximately 300,000 planes, 77,000 ships, 372,000 big guns, 20 million small arms, 6 million tons of bombs, 102,000 armored vehicles, and 2.5 million trucks. This output also aided Britain, Russia, and China through lend-lease. But we should acknowledge that lend-lease was not a one-sided arrangement. Giving guns to foreign soldiers saved American lives and helped to stop bombs from falling in American streets. Europe to the east and China to the west became America's first lines of defense. In return for equipment, America received important trade concessions and strategic British bases, which helped to establish America's postwar superpower presence around the world. And, through reverse lend-lease, Britain provided the United States with equipment and services, including access to military inventions.

Lend-lease was more important to Britain than to the Soviets. America contributed 25 percent of British equipment but only 4 percent of Russia's. Russian home production was massive, despite that the Germans captured or destroyed many plants. At its peak, Soviet industry turned out 40,000 planes and 30,000 armored vehicles a year, plus 150,000 big guns and 500,000 machine guns. Although many Soviet units initially had to fight with obsolete equipment, the increasing quality of Russian armaments surprised friends and enemies alike. The T-34 and heavier KV-85 tanks were a match for German Tigers and Panthers. When we add in that one of ten Russians died to destroy Hitler, we see that the Soviet contribution to the war effort was considerable.

America also produced much first-rate war matériel, such as the M-l rifle, a reliable shoulder arm. The proximity fuse, developed in 1943, used a tiny radio to detonate shells close to their targets, vastly improving, for example, the effectiveness of antiaircraft fire. However, other equipment was less impressive. The bazooka antitank weapon was inferior to the German Panzerfaust, taking two men to operate and leaving painful powder burns on the holder's face. American World War I–style automatic rifles were slower and clumsier than German light machine guns. The Spandau, for instance, was easily maintained and fired 1,200 rounds per minute, versus 500 for the Browning automatic rifle. Some U.S. antitank mines became unstable in subfreezing weather, with truckloads exploding in the severe winter of 1944–45. Submarine design at times lagged behind the Germans, whose boats were faster and featured a snorkel device that eliminated the need for surfacing at night to recharge batteries.

American and British tanks were largely weaker than German models in throw power (the weight of shell that could be fired) and armor thickness. The

Grant was mechanically unsound, and the thin 11-inch tracks of the Stuart sank in soft ground. The Sherman, although legendary as standard equipment for American and many British tank crews late in the war, had design deficiencies. Models with a gasoline, not a diesel, engine burned easily when hit: crewmen called them "the Ronson," after the cigarette lighter. The armor was thin and the 75-millimeter gun was outclassed by the German 88.

This weakness of Allied tanks was only partly an engineering fault. Military strategists shared culpability. The army's professional mindset was formed during the late nineteenth century, when mobile frontier forces battled the Plains Indians. This left a legacy of emphasizing speed at the expense of firepower and armor. As a result they favored faster, lighter equipment; conventional wisdom said it took five Shermans to kill a Panther. Without a tank powerful enough to thrust through enemy lines into the rear, Allied armor called in intensive air and artillery support to pound the enemy, helping to explain the brute force of much fighting in western Europe.

Reliance on blanket firepower rather than finesse as a primary tactical weapon was also encouraged by the abundance of U.S. resources. With plenty of ammunition, why not saturate everything ahead to save friendly lives? After 240-mm howitzers pounded the French town of Maizieres-les-Metz to eliminate German snipers, an American infantry surgeon "saw that it was in complete ruins, from one end to the other" (Colby, 269). French scholars estimate that to liberate Normandy, Allied forces killed about 70,000 civilians. Three thousand died on D-Day alone, about the same number as GIs killed.

Many Americans working in the arms industry were naive about the massive and often horrific destruction caused by modern weaponry. Unlike all other major belligerents, the United States was not a battleground, so civilians did not experience firsthand the awful effects of total war. A nurse on a plastic surgery ward back home might tend men with no eyes, noses, or mouths, and people working in war plants could suffer ill health from poor safety precautions, such as lung problems from fumes and cancer from chemicals that colored the skin orange. But Americans at home were neither bombed, burned, nor mutilated. Some failed to imagine what this might be like. There were jubilant parties in Washington, D.C., and other cities when the atomic bombs were dropped. One poll suggested 23 percent of Americans were disappointed that America had no more to drop. Soldiers who endured war's carnage were sometimes shocked to get letters from relatives asking eagerly how many enemy they had killed and urging them to get one more for the home folk.

Living apart from those who suffered firsthand, Americans were vouchsafed an ignorance of war's reality, allowing them to cherish an innocent belief that battlefield destruction was limited, that the weapons they made inflicted clean wounds, and that none they produced could be classified as inhuman or sordid. Most people felt no need to ponder whether the ends justified the means, as the means raised no moral qualms for them. Getting a job in the defense industry was simply getting ahead; you had no obligation to understand what the weapon you made was designed to do.

Commercials encouraged a complacent pride in war production. The government enlisted the advertising business to help sell the war, and Madison Avenue reminded people daily why the United States was fighting. However, advertising had inherent problems as an educational tool. By nature emotional rather than intellectual, it sold feelings rather than ideas. Content must be positive, so the consumer felt good about the product. As cultural historian John Costello commented, "If you want to sell a housewife Jell-O you don't tell her: 'Madam, it is highly probable that your son is coming home a basket case, or at least totally blind, but cheer up, tonight choose one of the six delicious flavors and be happy with America's finest dessert'" (Costello, 121).

Upbeat ads showed boyishly carefree air crews cheerfully relaxing with a coke after a bombing run, or a machine gunner (in a commercial for Talon zip fasteners, as useful to flyers as to housewives) giving the enemy hell from "a fish tank," the underbelly ball turret of a B-17 Flying Fortress. Fighting from a Plexiglas bubble thousands of feet up was actually a highly stressful experience, and the commercial omitted mentioning that if the plane's electrical system failed and the landing gear could not be lowered, the gunner would be crushed upon landing, knowing his fate the whole way down. Commercials encouraged affection for powerful weapons, associating them with popular consumer items from the same companies. Grim tools for maiming people, no matter how necessary, were transformed into innocuous tributes to American know-how, as benign as a new toilet bowl cleaner or pest control.

Take the flamethrower, which shot from a hose a jet of napalm or oil burning at 1,200°F or more. To the men who used it and suffered from it, this was a shocking if useful weapon for winkling out stiff resistance in caves, tunnels, and buildings. Veterans called it "hellfire." Men hit by the flame would flare up like Roman candles. The smell of roasted flesh was sickening. The body might burn for a whole day until only ash in human shape was left. So hated were the weapons that captured operators were usually executed outright by soldiers of every army. Ads deceived civilians as to this reality. One in the *New York Times* during February 1945 showed a flamethrower killing Japanese under the heading "Clearing out a rats' nest." Another said the flamethrower was "convincing the world of America's right to live the American way" (Fox, 69). The same message might have sold a new line of pickup trucks.

Many combat soldiers resented the distortion of the reality they endured, but in a media-dominated age, their views got buried. Advertising convinced civilians

that they were as informed about fighting, and pivotal to the war machine, as actual fighting men. "You are a *Production Soldier*: America's first line of defense," boomed one poster. "Give 'em both barrels," urged another, depicting a rivet gunner and a machine gunner as sharing the same frontline status. Ads implied that buying a war bond was a contribution on a par with military service. Even a boy collecting scrap iron became a media hero. The upshot, said distinguished journalist Eric Sevareid, was that Americans were sold the idea that wars are won by buying and selling, not by killing and dying (Sevareid, 215).

In World War II it became difficult to question defense spending and growth of the arms industry. During and after World War I there were those who warned against the growing role of weapons makers in national life. But, after America became the "arsenal of democracy" in the forties, massive defense contracts increasingly ceased to be controversial. The large corporation, once questioned as weakening individualism, emerged as a vital symbol of Americanism. The role was hammered home by advertising, which worked to connect brand-name manufacturing, American values, and world peace.

Americans now bemoan big government and federal intervention in all aspects of life, often without realizing that these phenomena were vastly magnified by World War II. Government agencies such as the War Production Board and the Office of Price Administration regulated economic and social life in the interests of the war effort. Government did a good job. But, at the same time, the central bureaucracy more than tripled. Big government worked closely with big business, which received the overwhelming majority of military contracts. These ties remained after the war ended, forming the embryo of the military-industrial complex that profoundly shaped American policy in the decades after the war. Joe Marcus, head of the Civilian Requirements Division during the war, reflected that "the single most important legacy of the war is . . . the military-industrial complex. In the past, there were business representatives in Washington, but now they *are* Washington" (Terkel, 326–27).

Along with burgeoning institutions came the concept of the organization society, in which the roles of individual intellect and conscience were diminished while loyalty to the group, being a team player, was emphasized. It seemed disloyal to criticize the government while the country was at war, so America's intellectuals voluntarily censored their doubts about such issues as area bombing, calls for exterminating the Japanese, and belligerent flag-waving. It felt wrong to obstruct in any way a cause that was so clearly right, even if this meant stifling qualms about national policies and attitudes.

Merle Curti, a student of American thought, noted that the war generated an aggressive nationalism, replacing the more self-critical, skeptical spirit of the thirties. Scientists developing weapons of mass destruction, including biological warfare and the atom bomb, worked behind a cloak of secrecy to preserve military security that precluded open and rational public debate about the wisdom of producing or using such weapons. Consequently, when President Truman thrust humanity into the nuclear age, nobody in the democracies had debated, much less voted on, the momentous issues involved.

The universities, normally sanctuaries for those whose vital role is to stand aside from the passions of the moment, having the intellect and training to take the long view and offer sensible second thoughts, undertook without question research projects that aided the war effort. Freedom of conscience, almost without notice, was curtailed and scholars became civilian soldiers in the military machine. Harvard, for example, became midwife to the birth of napalm. A postwar precedent was established for university professors, particularly in the sciences, to undertake government research for the military without assessing the purposes to which their work would be put. The surrender of individual moral responsibility in favor of national defense needs has roots in the war period.

The power of organized society to impinge upon the freedom of thought and action of the individual manifested itself in the selective service, which took men irrespective of their wishes. The draft was a highly effective tool for winning the war. In 1939, the army ranked forty-fifth in size in the world. But, by 1945, 16 million Americans had worn uniform, of whom 10 million, or just under two-thirds, were drafted. The belief that the World War II selective service was more fair than the Vietnam-era draft, causing much less resentment, is substantially correct. The 1940s draft cast a wider social net and resulted in a better balanced and possibly more mature fighting force than that of the 1960s. The first draftees were non-fathers aged twenty-one to thirty-five years. After July 1, 1943, eighteen-year-olds and some fathers were drafted. As a result, the average age was twenty-seven, versus nineteen for Vietnam.

Were World War II inductees well-adjusted because they understood that the attack on Pearl Harbor violated U.S. sovereignty, whereas in the 1960s Vietnamese communism never clearly threatened America? Perhaps. Also, 1940s draftees might have had less to lose, coming out of the Great Depression and a poor economic situation, than upwardly mobile young men of the 1960s, who gave up a potentially better domestic situation. This may have made some Vietnam-era inductees more resentful of military service.

At the same time, we should not take these kinds of comparisons too far because we can easily overstate the relative ideological commitment of the 1940s soldier, who often resented the government's power over his life. When the peacetime draft was introduced in 1940, calling for the induction of 80,000 men aged twenty-one to thirty-five, the legislation generated deep resentment and was excoriated as militarism. Although, in the following year, Congress extended the term of these men, the House approved the measure by only one vote, and many servicemen vowed to go "over the hill" in protest. Pearl Harbor changed this attitude, most drafted men now accepting their lot. There was even an initial rush to volunteer. But couples quickly married and conceived children as a stratagem to avoid service, initiating the baby boom. One official estimate attributed half the increase in marriages early in the war to people trying to avoid the selective service.

Some regular army officers, such as George Patton, thought that many draftees had less enthusiasm than inductees called up to fight in 1917–18. The recruits stumbled into draft boards drunk or with farewell hangovers. From there they marched glumly to the trains that took them to boot camp. In his novel of wartime life, *The Fall of Valor,* Charles Jackson described a party of New York inductees going to Grand Central Station to embark for a Southern camp. They were sheepish, shuffling, silent. "They straggled along hangdog and silly; they stared at the sidewalk in a ludicrous grin, or straight ahead, unseeingly" (Jackson, 20–21). Small boys jeered at them, echoing a long-standing tradition of street urchins mocking soldiers. One army wife, on a train with close-cropped recruits in their ill-fitting uniforms, felt like crying; they were "like freshly sheared sheep being led to a sheep dip" (Klaw, 14–15).

Waiting to hear if a family member's name had been drawn in the draft created daily tension and anxiety in households across the country. Ethel Gorham recalled, "You go through hell. Your husband's gloom, his constant irritation; the inability to carry on his job in the old routine fashion; your own restlessness and frustration . . . " (Weatherford, 265). Although actual draft evasion stood at a low 5 percent, many ordinary people still bitterly resented what they saw as class bias in the system. For example, college deferments, more than double those of 1917–18, seemed to protect society's privileged from equal sacrifice. One Bronx, New York, taxi driver, whose adolescent son had been taken, called his board "a bunch of crooks" who "don't touch those rich college kids" (Gervasi, 435). Such hostility increased as the deaths and mutilations of friends and family members mounted. On V-J night, when Japan surrendered, some draft board offices were defaced and vandalized.

In an era of virulent race prejudice, black Americans were inevitably victims of draft discrimination. Tennessee, for example, refused to put African Americans on draft boards, so that black inductees lacked sympathetic advocates of their own race to help them explain a legitimate domestic need for exemption from service. Blacks, especially in the South, could rarely afford to finish high school or go on to college, so they had no built-in shield against the draft, helping to explain why their deferment rate was lower than for whites. Persons of color were often denied conscientious objector status, the Black Muslim faith, for example, being officially rejected as a legitimate religion.

Conscientious objectors of all races, if fortunate enough to have their appeals accepted, might be incarcerated. They found there was no segregation in prison. But they were denied respect for their views, were treated as felons, and were harassed and sometimes beaten up by guards. There were about 18,000 conscientious objectors over the course of the war, a third of whom served prison terms; the others did civilian public service. It took a postwar Supreme Court decision for all conscientious objectors to get their civil rights back and expunge the felon label.

Some of the procedures used by selective service officers to rate draftees were of dubious reliability. Regarding the physical and mental condition of recruits, the statistics say that of 18 million men examined between 1940 and 1945, 29.1 percent were rejected as below induction standards. In the first year, 1940–41, a whopping 50 percent were flunked. Of these, 10 percent failed through illiteracy, the rest for psychological issues or physical defects such as bad teeth, poor eyesight, or venereal disease. As the need for men grew, the standards had to be lowered, and by 1943, many previously rejected men faced induction. Some draft officials and military officers complained that America was now scraping the bottom of the barrel.

Perhaps so, but we have reason to suspect that some methods of selection were flawed, partly because of subjective underlying assumptions. For instance, medical officers asserted that flabbiness among the eighteen to twenty-one age group presented a chronic problem. They were shocked to find that boys out of condition could not do ten squats; many had to be helped up after five. The findings provoked an almost hysterical overreaction among male physicians and psychologists, many of whom blamed the nation's mothers. They announced a national crisis of masculinity, an epidemic of "momism," brought on by women pampering their boys. In fact, more sober minds understood that most of these young men needed only the regimen of physical exercise provided by basic training and did not have to be rejected for service.

Thirty-two percent of rejections were made for psychological reasons, but these were based on as few as four standard, quite superficial, questions, including, "How do you feel?" "Do you like the army?" And, most questionable, "Do you like girls?" The boy who replied that the opposite sex intimidated him might be rejected as latently homosexual. Only America, of the belligerent nations, rejected men not for the overt commission of a homosexual act but for an alleged leaning in that direction. If a stripped recruit seemed uncomfortable with his nakedness, if he was a hairdresser or had effeminate gestures, he typically failed. A common joke was that if you wanted to avoid service, the easiest way out was to shave your armpits, wear perfume, and affect a mincing step at the physical exam.

Many recruiters came to what now appear simplistic judgments by placing unquestioning faith in behavioral science techniques still at a relatively early and crude stage of development. Practitioners suggested that you could quickly and easily process large masses of humanity through administering standardized questions. These researchers did not doubt their own objectivity, claiming the tests reflected a purely scientific outlook that took human error out of decision-making. Thus, you could detect a recruit who was latently homosexual simply by asking a correctly devised short question.

Actually, no standardized test was without inherent bias, and many reflected societal prejudices the questioner was unconscious of. Questions regarding sexual orientation were skewed by deep-seated homophobia. Reliance on standardized performance evaluations erased the individual: humanity was too complex to be measured quantitatively. Social scientists tried to apply industrial production-line quality-control techniques to people, assuming they could be graded like cans of peas. This was one of the worst aspects of the growth of the organization society, with its insistence on machinelike uniformity. And it hurt the performance of the army in the field.

Americans commonly believe that their World War II military was a rough-and-ready, can-do organization that won the war partly because it was more flexible and more innovative than its opponents, particularly the Germans. We stereotyped the Wehrmacht as hidebound Prussians fighting according to rigid, heel-clicking dogmas. The reality differed significantly. U.S. Army colonel Trevor N. Dupuy studied in-depth Allied versus German performance in the 1944 Normandy campaign. Despite complete Allied air superiority and massive numerical advantage on the ground, the enemy outfought us, inflicting a 50 percent higher casualty rate than they sustained. Similar findings led distinguished Israeli military historian Martin Van Creveld to compare German and American military structures as a way to understand the apparent disparity in fighting efficiency. The result was *Fighting Power* (1982), upon which I draw for much of the following discussion.

Van Creveld argued that Americans employed too much top-down direction, micromanaged issues best left to subordinates, and demanded obedience to orthodox rules and doctrine that robbed the frontline soldier of needed initiative. Too often he had to ask permission to call in fire or to exploit a situation in his immediate sector. In the navy, submarine commanders had to file a contact report and get permission to fire before engaging a surface vessel. This often meant the prey escaped.

Some Americans observed that discipline was poor among their men taken prisoner, compared to British or German POWs. They dealt badly with such matters as fair distribution of rations, arguments over food often degenerating into fistfights. They did not keep themselves clean and committed suicide at an abnormally high rate. This was partly because many junior officers had been allowed too little freedom of action to fully establish authority over the men without directives from above. When cut off by captivity from the normal functioning of organizational structure, many officers and noncoms lacked confidence in their own judgment and the experience to cope with unforeseen circumstances.

The Wehrmacht generally encouraged more initiative at the lowest levels, even on the part of private soldiers. It was expected that those on the ground would use their intelligence to exploit the immediate situation without losing time asking for direction from above. The American army, emphasizing behavioral science precepts of personnel management, was hierarchical, with rigid caste walls separating commissioned from enlisted ranks. The Germans, reversing our popular stereotype, were more structurally democratic, encouraging informal camaraderie between ranks and building a team spirit in which everyone mattered to the group.

Because the Wehrmacht employed less centralized management, less paperwork flowed up and down the chain of command. In the American army, every officer had to fill out a standardized, quantifiable report sheet on his subordinate officers each month, plus a fuller twice-yearly performance evaluation. This was obligatory even in combat. One infantry officer, sheltering in a shattered pillbox on the Siegfried line in February 1945, was about to grab some sleep when, "About midnight, a runner came up with a bunch of papers. I got under a blanket with a flashlight and found I was supposed to fill out an efficiency report on each officer who had been in the company during the past six months. I could not believe it" (Colby, 411).

The Germans asked only for an informal rating every two years, although a superior could intervene to remove a man from the field if he judged the situation warranted it. Men on the spot were expected to make sound professional decisions based on common sense. The result was that the American army developed a huge clerical staff to handle its enormous bureaucratic flow; by 1944, 35 percent of personnel were in clerical posts. The Wehrmacht had a much better teeth-to-tail ratio: in 1944, 54.35 percent of overall strength was in combat troops, versus 40.6 percent in the U.S. Army; 70 percent of German officers were in fighting units, in contrast to only 36 percent of American officers; many more Americans became staff officers, dealing with paperwork.

Emphasizing bureaucratic uniformity over practical application hurt individual personnel. Soldiers were typically issued a branch classification within two days, often on the basis of standardized aptitude tests assigning them to clerical, technical, infantry, or other status. Because the system functioned for the convenience of army administrators rather than the forces at the front, classifications were hard to change, even in an emergency. A field commander might have too few infantry, but he could not necessarily requisition fighters from a surplus of depot troops in the theater. His frontline units, through combat and exposure, might badly need relief, but he could not reassign fresher rear-echelon units to replace them. German field commanders utilized men as they saw fit, and classifications operated more as intelligent guidelines than as rigid categories.

Constant form-filling produced a tick-the-box-and-pass-it-on mentality. Confronted with the impossibility of trying to scientifically calibrate the performance of their subordinates each month, supervisors treated the forms as pro forma and ranked all officers in the top 25 percent. Thus, real problems with incompetent or exhausted officers did not always get dealt with. And for the GI in a combat unit, bureaucratic rigidity kept him in harm's way long after he needed a break.

The deep fog of paperwork, clogging communications channels, frustrated sharp responses to problems. Many American soldiers suffering the bitter north European winter of 1944–45 did so without protective clothing because their needs got lost in the pipeline. Lieutenant George Wilson, 4th Infantry Division, wrote, "No earmuffs, no hood, no face covering, no scarf" (Wilson, 205). There were also no protective liners for the ice-cold pot helmets, and the regulation issue wool gloves proved painfully inadequate. In another remarkable instance, the route of the USS Indianapolis, streaming to Guam in July 1945, got lost in the paper flow and for five days nobody knew the ship had been torpedoed and survivors needed rescuing.

In an army drawn from the democratic society with arguably the most personal freedoms on earth, egregious overmanagement caused friction. All military systems restrain individual freedom in the interests of molding effective collective behavior by the aggregate unit. But GIs often felt regulations went beyond the necessary to become petty tyranny, known colloquially as "chicken shit." Chicken shit could be refusing a soldier an off-base pass to visit his wife and newborn child in the local civilian hospital, or harassing a combat soldier on desperately needed R and R (rest and recreation) in a rear area for having dirt spots on his uniform or not saluting smartly enough. General George Patton was notorious for chicken shit: he would berate men on the front line for not wearing a tie or for having their trousers outside their leggings; he reputedly crept through latrines to catch and punish soldiers defecating without their helmets on.

Contrary to Hollywood movies, the army was not a big happy family of mutually respectful ethnic and class groups headed by universally beloved, fatherly officers. Intellectuals, who in films were happily surprised to find in army life a wonderful antidote to their previous unmanly existence of effete bookworming and whining social criticism, in reality often felt wretched and became appalled by their induction into military culture. Along with Jews, they were frequently the bait of training sergeants, who saw them as the privileged snobs of urban culture (nicely captured by army veteran Neil Simon in his 1988 play *Biloxi Blues*). Basic training, aimed at demolishing the recruit's civilian personality to rebuild him in the military's image, was hard on many but particularly rough on the educated. Herded together, stripped of the personal space crucial to privacy, shy or introspective men felt like animals, doing everything in public, from eating (like pigs at a trough, was one analogy) to urinating and defecating.

Very typically, during the early stages of the war, noncommissioned officers from the old regular army were less educated than the recruits under them, leading to mutual antagonism and frequent humiliation for the privates. Marine recruits were forced to march around the barracks with their gun in one hand and their penis in the other—or made to recite the correct way to kill a "Jap" by "a shot in the balls." The military machine strove to mold men into sameness. War correspondent John Steinbeck, watching soldiers file aboard a troopship in their round, potlike overseas helmets, thought they looked like so many mushrooms, vegetables bereft of individual identity. The soldiers learned that they did not count as individuals but were simply tools in the arsenal, so many "rifles" (according to Thomas R. St. George, who served in the Pacific). They knew that America would survive, but many of them, cogs in the war machine, would not.

For the better educated, conditions often improved after basic training, with opportunities for officer candidate school or assignment to a relatively safe, clean job in a technical or clerical division. For others, the tension and misery might continue, sometimes as a result of ethnic, gender, or class discrimination. All ethnic minorities were represented in the armed forces. Despite widespread public hostility to Hispanics, Mexican Americans volunteered in numbers far higher than their proportion of the population: 350,000 enlistees of a total 1.4 million did duty and won seventeen Congressional Medals of Honor. Thirty thousand Japanese Americans served, even though many of their parents were denied American citizenship and their families shipped to detention centers when they were drafted. A Japanese American unit in Europe became America's most decorated outfit. Out of a potential pool of 334,000 Native Americans, 29,000 served.

All of these minority groups faced some prejudice from the white majority, but at least many served in integrated regiments or divisions. This was good for their morale in most cases, though some Native Americans came home with confused identities, feeling neither mainstream nor simply Amerindian. However, in the case of African Americans, white loathing was so great that Jim Crow's rigid segregation followed the victims into the war machine. The buildup of the defense industries and the expansion of the armed forces on the eve of war were welcomed by blacks, who had endured a disproportionately high unemployment rate in the depression. But they immediately faced trials and disappointments. For some time, the U.S. Employment Service allowed employers to demand photographs from applicants to screen out persons of color. Those fortunate enough to get jobs in war industries usually found themselves in the lowest paid, most menial positions. Few achieved skilled or supervisory status. Conditions in the job market improved somewhat after a threatened protest march on Washington in 1941. But widespread discrimination continued, largely because the federal government would not enforce fair practices.

Discrimination in the armed forces bruised black personnel and damaged the war effort. Since the American and French revolutions, bearing arms had been associated with the right to claim full citizenship privileges. Black soldiers in the Civil War won the right to vote, although that right was systematically undermined after the war. In World War I, only France placed black U.S. doughboys alongside their own frontline troops and suitably honored their service. In 1941, influential whites did not intend to allow the black foot back in the political door, so they denied combat status to men of color. High-ranking officials, such as army chief of staff General George C. Marshall, were blunt about their belief in whites' racial superiority. Secretary of War Henry L. Stimson justified not appointing black officers on the grounds that "leadership is not embedded in the negro race." He also doubted that they had the brains to pilot planes, even though the 332nd Fighter Group, the Tuskegee Airmen, won a Presidential Unit Citation in March 1945.

More than a million blacks served, 8 percent of the total military. But 78 percent were in blue-collar service branches, compared to 40 percent for whites. For most of the war, the navy only allowed blacks on shipboard as mess boys (waiters). They were almost totally excluded from the air force, except for a few much publicized units, notably the 332nd, made noticeable by their scarcity value. Even the celebrated Ninth and Tenth Cavalry, black units whose fighting record went back to the Indian wars and San Juan Hill in Cuba, were dismounted from their tanks and put to work unloading ships, repairing roads, and driving trucks in North Africa.

To allay protest and preserve the military's image as a bastion of democracy, discussion of official discrimination was forbidden. Black soldiers' work was often dirty and dangerous: supply carriers went ashore right behind the first assault waves, road builders were exposed to artillery and sniper fire. But these jobs were neither glamorous nor in the public eye, making it hard to win decorations. One black veteran, who served in the quartermaster corps shifting supplies, recalled, "We were really stevedores. Many of those young blacks wanted to be in combat units" (Terkel, 275).

Late in the war, shortages of combat troops finally forced the administration to put black troops on the front lines, where they performed as well as white troops. African Americans finally received more than 12,000 decorations and citations. Even though blood donors were badly needed during the war, blacks' blood plasma was refused for white patients on the totally unscientific basis that it would "mongrelize" the Caucasian race. And, despite a nursing shortage late in the conflict, the services resisted recruitment of women of color; in 1945, of 60,000 nursing personnel, only 479 were black.

Jim Crow was unwieldy and expensive. Even in crisis situations, black officers could not command white soldiers. Not only black enlisted men but officers also could not dine with whites, frequent the same clubs, or use the PX (post exchange store). Several black soldiers were killed or wounded for trying to integrate army facilities. Others received dishonorable discharges for resisting discrimination. Racist white MPs beat up black soldiers and white girls caught together. Jim Crow was part of the dominant military culture, colluded in by those in authority.

The services also encouraged sexual and gender discrimination. Homosexual enlisted men who passed induction but were later spotted became targets of continuing persecution. (We are ignorant about homosexuality among commissioned officers, especially at the top, because American scholars, unlike Canadian researchers, have neglected this topic.) The services found lesbians somewhat less threatening, as there were fewer women in the forces, physical intimacy among females (such as kissing and touching) was more accepted in mainstream culture, and gay women were stereotyped as "butches" with masculine traits considered potential assets in the military. The military's preoccupation with rooting out homosexuals continued the witch-hunting prevalent within society at large, disrupting normal unit functions and provoking widespread unease.

Ironically, the rigidly sex-segregated structure of the armed forces brought homoeroticism closer to the surface. Men deprived of women's company resorted to sexual buffoonery, including all-male dances and cross-dressing skits at impromptu theatricals, activities frowned on before the war. Enforced same-sex intimacy, such as sleeping in overcrowded beds at facilities in embarkation ports, or hugging each other in foxholes to keep warm, could result in "deprivation homosexuality." Loneliness, grief over the loss of buddies or hospital patients, the simple need for human consolation and affirmation of life among war's miseries, led service personnel of both genders to embrace gay encounters. For heterosexuals, these were brief interludes, without larger significance. But in war's extraordinary circumstances, some discovered in themselves a latent homosexuality leading to long-term gay commitment. For example, Donald Vining, a YMCA volunteer, admitted to having many sexual encounters with male GIs using his facilities, not all of them confirmed homosexuals. They transformed his life, enabling him to discover his true sexual orientation.

Men caught and found guilty of occasional homosexual offenses got a dishonorable discharge, blocking veterans' benefits and career advancement in civilian society. Repeat offenders got heavy prison sentences, often stretching over a decade. The treatment of the accused was traumatizing: suspects were chained, forced to wear special labels, and put in stockades where MPs often mentally and physically abused them. They were tried before boards without legal counsel. By war's end, about 10,000 had been condemned, stripped of medals and honors, and disgraced at home, their local draft boards receiving notification of adverse court martial findings.

The pursuit of gays wasted time and resources. There was no proven correlation between sexual preference and military performance. In fact, members of the military repeatedly acknowledged the efficiency of homosexual personnel. On one American warship, the best torpedo officer reputedly was "a notorious Queen" who wore a hair net and bathrobe, even in action. Given that 10 percent of any nation's males are usually homosexual, the services reduced their potential manpower pool. Moreover, many gays had a higher than normal ideological commitment to the war, since the Nazis had targeted homosexuals for liquidation. Rejection of American homosexuals negated their patriotism and idealism.

It may surprise us to learn that irrespective of sexual preference, women of all ethnic groups faced significant public antipathy for wanting to join the military. Overall, 350,000 women served in the forces: 150,000 in the army, 100,000 in the navy, 22,000 in the marines, and thousands more in the Coast Guard and the reserves. But, especially at first, the solidly white male civil and military establishment resented the female presence as implying that men alone could not protect America. One congressman fumed, "Think of the humiliation! What has become of the manhood of America?" (Costello, 41). Yet it soon became clear that with the high rejection rate of male inductees, America needed women in uniform to help staff the bureaucracy.

In 1943 the army undertook a massive recruiting campaign to enlist half a million women. As an incentive, for the first time in army history, women would receive the same pay and benefits as male soldiers, including veteran's entitlements (a promise later forgotten). The WACs, or Women's Army Corps, did as well as men in the areas allotted to them. General Eisenhower relied heavily on WACs as staff personnel in planning and communications. There were 8,000 WACs on the European mainland when Germany surrendered. In the Pacific, MacArthur praised them as among his best soldiers for their hard work and good discipline. Yet women at no time represented more than 2 percent of the military machine, and service for females failed to gain mainstream acceptance.

Why? To begin with, the military retained traditional American views of gender separation. America alone refused to place women in battle zones. In

Europe and Asia, for example, women fought and died both in uniform and in the resistance movements. Most U.S. females in uniform were restricted to typically low-level "woman's work," such as typing or, for black women, mopping floors and emptying waste baskets. The percentage of women who filled clerical posts in the military was greater than in civil life. Reflecting patriarchal culture, female officers could not issue orders to male personnel. Married women were not welcome, and their families were denied the normal dependency allowance. Pregnant soldiers got automatic discharges. So did menopausal personnel, because male officers, scientifically ignorant, thought this natural biological change permanently incapacitated women.

Females faced promotion ceilings and other bars to professional advancement. Although nurses were desperately needed, the Senate refused to apply the principle of selective service to women. Black women were kept out of the defense industry and, when they complained, were referred to situations as domestic servants. Most nursing schools refused admission to black women, and the army let them tend only black soldiers. The navy begrudgingly accepted four black nurses.

The media patronized professional women. Press reports consistently dubbed WACs the "Petticoat Army" and their quarters "Fort Lipstick." Even good war reporters like Ernie Pyle condescended to them, calling them "gals," and any story about women in the field included an obligatory reference to their giggly ways and their "frilly panties" hanging on washing lines by the tents. The demeaning of women was pervasive enough that the official War Department *Guide to Great Britain* (1942), issued to GIs bound for the United Kingdom, warned them not to take their attitude overseas.

Britain was the first belligerent to conscript females, starting in 1942. Women in uniform helped defend Britain against the Luftwaffe, serving in command centers and radar stations that came under frequent air attack. Both royal princesses Elizabeth and Margaret served. Campaign ribbons on females' military blouses were earned. British respect for their female troops was such that nobody thought women officers commanding men seemed funny or inappropriate. The *Guide* told American troops that treating these personnel with disrespect would earn them the enmity of the British and a possible bloody nose.

Some Americans could not imagine women making a military contribution beyond giving sexual favors to male personnel: there were pervasive rumors stateside of immorality among servicewomen, and it was even said they staffed brothels for officers. Surveys showed that 90 percent of GIs bought into these rumors. The military brass nurtured the culture of misogyny. For example, if a man and woman in uniform were caught having sex, she was punished but he was not, on the assumption she must be the instigator. A woman might be dishonorably discharged for sexual promiscuity while a male had to commit an actual crime to face the same penalty.

GI hostility to female personnel was increased by the military caste system. For example, the bulk of female medical personnel, who served in all theaters of war, held commissioned rank. By regulation, only male officers, not enlisted men, could date them. In the sex-starved atmosphere, this created resentment resulting in sexual assaults. We should know more about these cases, but the Pentagon resisted investigation or disclosure. The military very often failed to take appropriate action in rape cases, the victim being blamed for "encouraging" the male's behavior, an attitude that continues today.

The crude stereotyping of female military personnel as morally loose hurt recruiting, as women shied away from being smeared. But the most important factor in holding back female recruitment was that enlisted women often took rear-echelon slots that might otherwise be available to save men from frontline service. Women were reluctant to join up when doing so might send a man to die. Evelyn Fraser, a WAC, recalled, "When we came along, the men in clerical jobs were none too happy. We replaced them for combat overseas." The feeling against women serving was not helped by the WAC recruiting slogan, "Release a man for combat" (Terkel, 123).

Many men, understandably, did not want a combat posting. Some frontline infantry resented the disproportionate share of hardship and sacrifice they bore. As most black males and all women were barred from combat, and better educated white males might get desk or technical jobs that were comparatively safe, a disproportionate share of fighting and dying fell to underprivileged and unskilled white males. The infantry had the lowest prestige of any service; it got maximum risk with minimum compensation. The air force, marines, and paratroops offered glamor along with the danger. White men whose scores were in the bottom half of the Army General Classification Test were assigned to the "foot sloggers." This does not mean that American infantry were not of a high overall caliber, or lacked pride in being fighting men, but some demoralization and surliness became inevitable. An army study showed that many combat troops were not the happy-go-lucky boyish warriors pictured by the media.

This seminal study was carried out by the Information and Education Division of the army, under the leadership of sociologist Samuel A. Stouffer. His team found that infantry scored lowest on morale, combat soldiers often feeling they had a rotten deal. Seventy-five percent of frontline troops wanted to be replaced and repatriated. Most admitted they would avoid more combat if they could, a safe (nonmutilating) wound being the preferred ticket out. The study concluded, with notable candor, that two factors held men in the lines. Coercion was one, especially as soldiers did not want dependents losing their pay and benefits subsequent to court martial. Second, they stayed for their buddies: "Our bunch of GIs was not fighting for mother, country, and apple pie," said Sergeant John Babcock, 78th Infantry Division. "Our ties were to those unfortunates fighting next to us, sharing the same fate" (Babcock, 54).

Among the people the fighting men hated, according to Paul Fussell, a veteran of the European theater, were civilians, rear-echelon troops, including staff officers, seen as shirkers or, worse, and black marketeers who stole supplies intended for combat troops. Combat veterans asked why base clerks got the same campaign ribbons they did? Joe Hanley, an infantry veteran, recalled the sense that he was cannon fodder, willingly sacrificed by a society glad to get him out of the labor pool: "Nobody really cared about you whatsoever. It was a big surprise to everybody when you came home. What are you doing here?" they asked (Terkel, 273).

Servicemen in general shared the infantry's alienation from civilians. They made far less money than people living safely at home and getting ahead while griping about bad coffee and gas shortages. Striking workers were loathed by GIs, along with manufacturers who risked soldiers' safety by cheating on armor thickness or quality of weapons' parts. Servicemen were also made uneasy by reports of sliding moral standards. One soldier returning from leave claimed, "Everything's in a mess. Busiest people after this shindig will be the divorce lawyers" (Murphy, 235). One infantry officer wrote home, "Every day or so a soldier comes in and tries to find out how he can stop his allotment to his wife or get a divorce. So many of the wives are doing their husbands wrong" (Litoff, 209).

Movies gave many civilians false impressions of high idealism at the front. Hollywood usually had a leading character in each war film deliver an inspiring speech on why he was fighting. Richard Leacock, who served in Burma, said of these pictures: "I remember those Hollywood films where people sat in their trenches and had ideological discussions about the beauties of democracy at home. Oh bullshit!" (Terkel, 376). Indeed, according to Stouffer's team, only 13 percent of GIs could name three of the four freedoms America was fighting for, while 33 percent knew none. (Announced by FDR in August 1941, they were: freedom of speech and of religion, freedom from want and fear.) Ernie Pyle saw no reaction among GIs to the news that the Senate had ratified the establishment of the United Nations; it appeared irrelevant to their world.

The army tried to boost ideological commitment through an orientation program, including the *Why We Fight* film series. But much material, delivered in lectures by uncomfortable or incredulous junior officers, seemed simplistic, even condescending. For example, Hitler was compared to a bullying small-town major trying to dictate how to raise your kids or where you could work. British and French troops determined to effect major postwar social reform in return for their sufferings, particularly as a disproportionate share of bombs had fallen on working-class districts where the underprivileged lived. They talked of redistributing wealth to achieve universal health and welfare benefits. Most American troops, when surveyed, asked for no such social changes. They just wanted to get home to a piece of the action, defined as a good job and a new car. Songs popular in the services, such as "Don't Sit under the Apple Tree" or "White Christmas," reflected a simple longing for normality.

William Manchester, a marine who fought in the Pacific, said his was not a rebellious generation. No counterculture existed, and people conformed readily, fearing class warfare. Perhaps they were right to doubt that proclaiming four freedoms would ultimately amount to anything. They knew the war had to be won, but it was a job, not a crusade. "I have very few ideals in this war. If there's a Jerry tank firing at me or my buddies, I want to bring artillery fire on him," Joseph E. Garland, 145th Infantry Division, wrote in his diary, April 29, 1944. "Anything else is out of this world. If the soldier votes—good—if he doesn't, so what. He's a political tool at best" (Garland, 234).

Felt obligation to the war effort dropped sharply among men in battle zones as victory neared in 1944–45. This was particularly true in Europe, as Germany crumbled. The sense was, "Hey, most people now, especially back home, are going to make it through this war and live happily ever after. Why should I get shot at this stage in the game?" Many men went absent without official leave (AWOL). Paris and other major cities filled with them. In all, about 40,000 soldiers deserted during the war; 2,854 were court-martialed, and at least one was shot. Not all deserters simply decided they wanted to survive the war. Throughout hostilities, from 1941 to 1945, men broke involuntarily under the terrible strain of combat. When, in the next chapter, we look at the reality of battle, we shall see why soldiers might have breakdowns or be driven to run away.

CHAPTER FOUR

Overseas

When Americans went overseas in World War II, they entered a much wider world than most had experienced, or could even have imagined. Many encounters with other peoples, off the battlefield, were mutually affirming and broadened the Yanks' perspectives. At the same time, the experience of combat proved harsh and often sordid. And while most military personnel acted with decency and restraint abroad, some abused or committed crimes against those who came within their power. A minority besmirched the uniform by running well-organized black-market operations that included large-scale theft of U.S. military property.

The public at home was largely shielded from this darker reality. Full disclosure of what happened overseas was considered bad for morale and therefore censored by the government and media. Thus, when Ernie Pyle reported the soldiers wanted to "make love to" Olga, who broadcast anti-Allied propaganda from Berlin, he was using a euphemism for rape. Civilians preserved an image of their "boys" as innocents who did not swear, drink, or commit crimes. Even though *fuck* was the most common noun, verb, and adjective in the military vocabulary, the *U.S. Infantry Journal*, dutifully conforming to public sentiment, officially tut-tutted the use of profanities. American mothers, delicately ignoring the killing work their sons were sent overseas to do, formed organizations to worry the army about the boys' morals in such areas as sex, drinking, and gambling. The army responded by denying alcohol to the ranks.

* * *

Many GIs just arriving overseas did, in fact, look and act very young. Europeans noted that some behaved "as if they were children," incessantly chewing gum, playing ball in the street, guzzling Cokes, and reading shallow comic books. They seemed immature, as they had not grown up amid war and because their parents had worked to prolong in them the sheltered innocence that Americans treasured as a national asset. Away from home and normal restraints, they often acted with an unconcern that was refreshing, yet the naive mental set could transform into something more troubling.

War is inherently destructive, and this characteristic can have a sinister attraction. Constructing a building is creative, but it takes patience, ability, and training. Crushing a building can also seem creative, in a secondhand way, but it can be done quickly by someone with little talent. This is why children smash toys they otherwise cannot handle: they try to perform through crushing. "The way I messed up that house was beautiful," says a machine gunner in veteran Harry Brown's *A Walk in the Sun*. "I could do that fifty times a day" (Brown, 166). An infantry lieutenant who got to fire a 155-mm howitzer found that the massive blast thrilled him, making his carbine seem like a toy.

The sense of omnipotence powerful weapons lent to soldiers was not unique to Americans, but two factors exacerbated the destructive urge in Americans. First, the juggernaut of the U.S. war machine produced earth-moving machinery, such as bulldozers, and heavy munitions that blasted the landscape in such quantities that they profoundly changed the environment. Second, Americans, who had spent centuries clearing virgin land, had less interest in preservation than other peoples who lived in amity with the natural features and ancient architecture of their homelands.

The British, to protect their rural environment, built military facilities around landscape features so that, for example, air bases coexisted with farms, fields, and woods. Americans used their powerful machinery to scrape the earth bare and then put their facilities flat on the landscape: "ugly, barren, temporary . . . bases that had been nailed together overnight," as one U.S. soldier remembered (Baker, 269). Herman Wouk commented on the Pacific: "With the coming of the Americans, the once-tropic islands had taken on the look of vacant lots in Los Angeles" (Wouk, 351). Eric Sevareid worried about the potent combination of green American youth, powerful technology, and insensitivity to nature. The GIs "had the minds of simple children," he thought, "but their hands were wizards' hands." Like "a blind Gulliver," they swept up fragile Lilliputian peoples and places, scooping out the earth with giant mechanical fingers (Sevareid, 233).

Americans in Asia, like other Westerners, acted with racial arrogance. They mostly behaved better in Europe, but some still exhibited an aggressive ethnocentricity. Most had no interest in learning from other peoples and lived only to get back home. Their greatest loathing was for Arabs, whom they met in North

Africa, and for Asians of the Pacific region. But they even held the British and French in contempt for their rationed food or their lack of consumer goods and modern appliances, such as refrigerators. And they often doubted their Allies' fighting qualities because they could not beat the Axis without American aid.

Imbued with condescension, a minority of Americans acted badly, feeling that the rules of good behavior applied only at home. They festooned trucks with blown-up rubbers (contraceptives), and threw packs of condoms or candies at passing civilians. They looted or stole, for which they were frequently punished, even executed, if the crimes happened in friendly territory. But their misdemeanors were often overlooked in Italy, Germany, and Japan, where such robbery was termed "liberation" of enemy property. Some enthusiastically took part in the black market, which burgeoned, especially in Europe, as the war progressed. Huge quantities of supplies bound for U.S. fighting forces were stolen by Americans themselves. For example, they fleeced one-third of all supplies landed in Naples for the Italian front. In one episode, a whole train of material was hijacked.

Some white GIs, especially from the Southern states, took their racial prejudices overseas and demanded that other people conform to their views, wrecking bars, restaurants, and other businesses that served black troops along with white. The British, although prejudiced against their own colonial ethnic troops, accepted black Americans simply as GIs. But the U.S. Army insisted that facilities catering to their troops in Britain be formally segregated. British girls who dated black soldiers might be beaten up, and several of their escorts were killed, by either white GIs or MPs who typically blamed black personnel for provoking incidents by overstepping American racial boundaries.

Sexual relations are a problem whenever any nation's soldiers are away from home. Americans in both world wars worked hard to keep the boys pure. The post office confiscated too-explicit pinups mailed to soldiers. Purity groups fought the issuance of prophylactics (naively assuming that without condoms the men would abstain) or the organization of official brothels under proper medical supervision. USO shows were expected to keep troops wholesomely entertained without sex. The military had to treat the reality of sex as a covert operation. For example, the establishment of prophylactic stations close to approved brothels in rest areas had to be kept secret. John Steinbeck reported that the shipments of rubbers for these establishments had to be disguised in the States as devices "to keep moisture out of machine-gun barrels—and perhaps they did" (Steinbeck, 4). In Britain, the government and the American military finally cooperated in a sex-education campaign that brought the venereal disease rate down by 66 percent.

But, too often, American authorities were handicapped by home-front pressure to preserve the illusion of innocence at the expense of pragmatic intervention, hurting military efficiency. One Indian newspaperman branded GIs as VD-ridden seducers of women. Venereal disease cases did, indeed, soar when U.S. troops came to town. In the northern European theater, VD caused more American casualties than the German V2 rocket. At one point in the Italian campaign, venereal infections outweighed battlefield wounds. In France, the rate went up 600 percent after the liberation of Paris, Allied soldiers taking sex as their reward.

Because war is inextricably bound up with death, and knowledge of mortality produces a need to affirm life, the procreative act becomes central for those making war. Soldiers had sex wherever and whenever possible: 50 percent of married and 80 percent of single men in uniform admitted to having casual intercourse. GIs fathered tens of thousands of illegitimate children in Britain. In war-ravaged locales like Rome, Naples, Paris, Berlin, Manila, and Tunis, they took advantage of females' desperate need for food, tobacco, and clothing to barter goods for sex. Peter Belpulsi admitted, "For a pack of cigarettes, a GI in Paris didn't have any trouble to find a prostitute" (Belpulsi, 174).

Unchanneled sexual need produced rape. One recent estimate suggests that as many as 18,000 U.S. rapes occurred in Europe alone. Motives for sexual assault included male bonding (40–50% of assaults were gang rapes), an enhanced sense of masculine power, and revenge against the enemy. The judge advocate general warned that, as the armies advanced into enemy territory, the situation became ripe for violent sex crimes, resulting in an avalanche. For example, in the ten-day period between August 30 and September 10, 1945, there were up to 1,300 rape cases in Japan's Kanagawa province alone.

But women were not safe even in Allied countries. GIs in France raped at least 2,500 women, French girls being stereotyped as morally loose and therefore "asking for it." American soldiers treated Australian women so badly that two pitched battles with Aussie troops ensued. Inevitably, given white American attitudes to black male sexuality, African American GIs were punished more severely for alleged rapes. Although making up only 10 percent of the forces, they represented about 65 percent of those punished for sex crimes (by contrast, only 14 percent of those punished for desertion were black).

Alcohol was officially denied to boys on base. It must be the ultimate act of willful naïveté to pretend that a man engaged in killing other men will be morally corrupted by a bottle of booze. Only the American army tried to keep its ranks dry (though, because of the military caste system, the prohibition excluded officers). The result was an army obsessed with obtaining liquor. Whiskey became a form of currency, with a fixed value in trading for other items; a Samurai sword, for example, was worth so many bottles. Those without the wherewithal for barter distilled their own substitutes. Aqua Velva aftershave from the PX and grapefruit juice made a piquant cocktail reminiscent of a Tom Collins. A five-gallon can of fruit and a handful of sugar, left in the sun to ferment, made a cloying but potent brew called "swipe." A similar concoction, involving coconut and raisins, produced vicious hangovers. The less inventive drank medical alcohol or torpedo fluid, risking blindness or death.

Some troops also scrounged pep pills and got hooked on them. At least 10 percent of American troops took amphetamines at some time. Benzedrine was very popular; 25 percent of men in the stockade (field prison) were heavy users. Morphine, used as a pain killer, produced addiction among thousands of wounded. Deprivation of narcotic substances tended to produce obsession with the object of denial. Paul Fussell, a veteran of the European theater, said the infantry's canteens contained booze as often as water.

Most American civilians did not understand the nature of battle and so were oblivious to what soldiers encountered. Combat could be exhilarating. War got men away from the humdrum, workaday world and stimulated an adrenaline flow rare in civilian life. Personal issues were crystalized: live or die. Soldiers spoke of team spirit and camaraderie often absent in the competitive marketplace. Some never lost their taste for fighting. But for the average man, prolonged exposure to combat became physically and mentally debilitating. About 25–30 percent of casualties were psychological cases; under very severe conditions that number could reach 70–80 percent. In Italy, 54 percent of wounds were emotional. On Okinawa, under nightmarish conditions, 7,613 Americans died, 31,807 sustained physical wounds, and 26,221 experienced mental damage.

The symptoms of combat breakdown varied. A man suffering from shell shock, diagnosed in World War I (shattered nerves and potential brain damage from prolonged exposure to the concussions of artillery bombardment), might display an abnormal sensitivity to noise and sudden light, the characteristics of an exploding round, and become helpless. A psychiatric casualty in North Africa said, "I just want to be where it's quiet; I don't want to ever hear a gun again" (Wecter, 546). Some mentally ragged men were wracked by stomach pains and migraines. An early warning signal was the "two thousand yard stare," a vacant expression fixed on the far horizon, accompanied by a steep decline in spirits, even loss of the urge to self-preservation. Men might intuit they were close to the edge of sanity. They hallucinated the dead coming back to life, wept unaccountably and uncontrollably, or became prey to morbid fears such as that they would run amok, killing their comrades. Without medical attention, they sometimes did.

In the face of all evidence to the contrary, even experienced military men clung stubbornly to the fiction that only cowards broke down; heroes did not. Psychi-

The Anguish of Combat. Drawing by Howard Brodie.
Courtesy of the U.S. Army Center of Military History

atric cases were often branded "mommies' boys," spoiled brats. General George Patton, who slapped two patients hospitalized for chronic stress, declared belligerently, "Americans pride themselves on being he-men and *are* he-men" (Farago, 231). Actually, one man Patton hit had fought through North Africa and Sicily but faltered after a friend was badly wounded and his wife delivered a baby he feared he would not live to see.

This example exposes the popular fallacy that men who survived their first dose of fire became battle-seasoned and would be fine from then on out. In fact, there was no such thing as getting acclimatized to combat; the more exposure, the more likely the incidence of breakdown. The attempt to divide men into heroes and cowards avoided some major complexities: a man might be steadfast on a beach but crack up in street fighting; he might be able to hold up under shelling yet go to pieces in a dive-bomber attack. Sometimes, heroics came from exhaustion and hopelessness: you wanted the enemy to kill you to end the misery.

The charge that men who failed in combat had grown up dominated by women, tied to mom's apron strings, was examined by the Stouffer team of army researchers. They found no evidence that psychiatric casualties had more possessive mothers. They did, however, perceive a linkage between childhood lessons and distress over taking life. Parents and spiritual authorities taught kids that killing was a sin. The more indelibly youngsters absorbed this lesson, the more traumatizing would be the taking of life. Later wartime patriotic admonitions that killing in uniform was admirable could not always overcome earlier prohibitions.

The soldiers' moral qualms helped to account for a phenomenon that some army field research teams thought they observed: only a minority of riflemen fired their weapons in battle; sometimes as few as 25 percent. The bulk of mayhem, it appeared, was inflicted by heavy weapons platoons, artillery, and aircraft that released missiles from way off, distancing the killing act. In 1947, the army's chief combat historian, S. L. A. Marshall, caused a national scandal when he placed the 25 percent figure before the general public in a highly readable book, *Men against Fire.* The resulting debate led to the military changing the way men were trained on the rifle range.

Marshall's revelations have been consistently controversial. His research methods and field interview techniques have been assailed, and some veterans resented his argument as a slur. Harold Leinbaugh, a company commander in the 84th Infantry Division, said few, if any, men failed to shoot their weapons. However, in 1995, army psychiatrist Dave Grossman, in *On Killing*, asserted that the rate of fire in rifle companies only went up dramatically in the Vietnam War era, after the military changed from the World War II passive training with a bull's-eye target to life-size pop-up human effigies trainees were expected to shoot on instantaneous reflex. This "fire, don't think" approach overcame built-in prohibitions against killing.

Whatever the case, there is no question that, for many World War II combatants, killing did carry with it grave psychological aftereffects. When marine William Manchester shot his first Japanese, a sniper who had to be eliminated, he nevertheless threw up and wet his pants, crying and repeatedly telling the corpse that he was sorry. A man might rationalize death because the enemy was evil. Thus, soldiers often had little difficulty accepting the demise of German SS troopers, seen as ruthless thugs. Still, the problem remained: most Germans looked like, bled like, and smelled like Americans. It was somewhat easier to kill the Japanese (the fire rate in the Pacific was slightly higher than in Europe) because they seemed more different and, unlike the Germans, were known to have committed widespread atrocities upon Americans.

The fighting man was also caught morally between competing and incompatible demands upon him. To be of use to his family dependents, a man had to survive to provide for them; to serve his nation, he had to be willing to die. Tension between these conflicting loyalties produced nervous breakdowns. However, the most important reason for the relatively high breakdown rate among American troops (in the German army it averaged 2–2.7%) was the classification system (discussed in chapter 3) that put the whole weight of death-dealing on a small percentage of men designated irrevocably for combat.

With no effective limit to his term of service, a rifleman was likely to stay in the infantry until he was killed, badly wounded, cracked up, or the war ended. Combat infantry suffered about 90 percent of a division's battle injuries (versus, say, 5% for the artillery). As only a minority of new recruits joined the infantry, men at the front could not be given even short breaks and might be on the line constantly for weeks. Any brief rest they got could be no more than a hundred yards from the front. To alleviate the situation, a policy was introduced allowing theater commanders to rotate a limited number of men home each month. But combat needs meant that normally far fewer than the allotted number could be spared; the constant dashing of hope for relief added to demoralization and combat fatigue.

General Omar Bradley complained, "The rifleman trudges into battle knowing that the odds are stacked against his survival. He fights without promise of either reward or relief" (Holmes, 261). The odds Bradley was talking about were these: in three months of combat, an infantry regiment might suffer 100 percent casualties. The sense of doom could lead to self-destructive behavior, like that of marines in New Guinea who played Russian roulette—gambling on who would be blown away by the one round in a pistol chamber, revolved before each player put the gun to his head and fired. In this macabre mortality play, you might as well exit one way as another. Alternately, unable to stand any more fighting, a man might desert. The U.S. officially acknowledged 50,000 desertions during the war, of which 80 percent were combat infantry.

Further organizational errors compounded morale problems. U.S. divisions should have been smaller so they could be rotated out of the line without causing huge gaps at the front. Replacements could then have joined the divisions at rest and trained with them, becoming fully integrated members of the team before exposure to combat. As it was, rookies were often thrown into action with no chance to adjust to their situation. Veterans who had healed from previous injuries should have been returned to their old outfits, not sent randomly to strange units. For bureaucratic convenience, all replacements, including recovered wounded, went into a central pool and were fed piecemeal into the line, where they were often resented as outsiders by the old-timers, who allotted them the most dangerous assignments to protect their buddies. Some of the least necessary deaths, physical and emotional wounds, resulted from men being thrown into the meat grinder, friendless and unsupported.

The result of keeping troops at the front too long was an inevitable drop in combat efficiency. A soldier in the line for, say, ten days would reach a maximum level of experience and competence. This would sustain through about the next twenty-five days. After that, his usefulness would decline until, after sixty days, he would be worn out, and by seventy or so he often needed hospitalization. Some of the 146th Engineers, who fought to exhaustion against the Germans in November 1944, were said to be like broken violin strings, overstretched for too long. Inexorably, the hero of ten days became the "coward" of eighty days whom Patton slapped. One arrested deserter, who had fought through Africa, Sicily, Italy, and southern France, said all the men he had trained with were killed. Promised repatriation, his rotation never came. "I can't stand the infantry any longer. Why won't they transfer me to some other outfit?" (Gray, 17).

What was it about action that brought a man to this pass? Combat was not like the wartime Hollywood movies that presented a sanitized, romanticized version of battle. Admiral Gene LaRocque, an experienced fighting man, said: "I hated to see how they glorified war. In all those films, people get blown up with their clothes and fall gracefully to the ground. You don't see anybody being blown apart. . . . You see only an antiseptic, clean, neat way to die gloriously" (Terkel, 189).

If it was not antiseptic, neat, and clean, what was combat? What was it that made madness or desertion the last defense against the combatants' surroundings? Let us accompany the fighting forces overseas. Stress began with the troopship that took men away from America, for most their first break from home. The sense of being a herd of animals marked for slaughter began on the outward-bound voyage. Loneliness was intense, particularly among married men, who knew they might not see their wives and children again. They might develop "nostalgia," a debilitating psychosomatic illness that twinned homesickness with loose bowels and might require hospitalization.

Troopships were often modified merchantmen, their holds full of stark scaffolding that converted cargo space into acres of bunks reaching into the upper darkness of the cavernous metal tombs. Passengers might have to climb ladders to reach beds twelve or more levels high. These conditions produced chronic claustrophobia that men struggled to control. Holds retained the rotting smells of previous cargoes that, combined with the roll of the ship, made men sick, so they stank, too. The ill vomited on those below. When possible, the decks were flushed with hoses, but this was difficult because, if too many men were cleared to one side of the ship to cleanse the other, the change in weight could make the boat capsize and roll over. Anxiety was pervasive, as ships at sea were rife with rumors: a U-boat wolf pack was assembling to sink the convoy or a deadly epidemic was sweeping the boat.

Sooner or later, troopships would take the men to a hostile landing on a foreign beach. Often, belts and ties were taken from the particularly young or excitable the night before disembarkation; one female nurse said, "They were very, very young. In their fearful anticipation, they might do themselves damage" (Terkel, 286). Foot soldiers dreaded the beaches because they maximized the worst features of combat. A man would climb down the ship's netting to the assault boat, often in a pitching sea, carrying 85 to 135 pounds of equipment. If he missed his footing and plummeted into the water, he would sink and drown.

Landing craft, chugging slowly toward the shore, were sitting ducks. On board, most troops were silent; some wept, others vomited. In a beach landing, the inconceivable happened. At Kuralei, a direct shell hit flung a barge of men high in the air, and the boat came down on them. The few who survived were shot in the water by Japanese snipers. Going ashore in southern France, during landings following D-Day, Lieutenant J. Glenn Gray saw the boat next to his blown apart, scattering flesh and bone everywhere. The shock made a fellow officer lose his voice for three days. At Tarawa, a coxswain went mad from piloting his boat through body parts run after run. And a wounded battalion commander who crawled onto a pile of bodies to avoid drowning in the surf was recovered the next day, insane. To make an emotionally shattered naval officer take his men close enough to wade ashore on D-Day, platoon commander Elliott Johnson shoved his pistol in the man's mouth. When the landing ramp came down, machine-gun cross-fire from both ends of the beach cut in half many trying to disembark before they could go five yards; even the lightly wounded drowned in the surf.

The shore line was a surreal hell. Ernie Pyle said the D-Day coast for a mile out was littered with shattered boats, tanks, trucks, rations, packs, buttocks, thighs, torsos, hands, heads. Hostile fire swept the beach, creating more confusion and casualties among the men, who naturally went to earth in the face of such carnage. Young soldiers bunched together, some crying or soiling themselves. Timuel Black, an African American GI unloading equipment on Utah Beach, recalled there were "young men crying for their mothers, wetting and defecating themselves. Others tellin' jokes," unreasonable jocularity also being an emotional response to horror (Terkel, 276).

The men had to be forced forward, off the beaches. Conventional theory in World War II held that fear was natural, but you must not give in to it; you had to move forward before hostile fire found you. This tactic usually made sense. But in the days and months that followed the initial landings, the troops would force themselves to get up and push forward over so many naked expanses, each time expecting death, that finally putting one foot ahead of the other became an act of heroic will. And one day, the feet would no longer respond on command.

> I must lie down at once, there is
>   a hammer at my knee.
> And call it death or cowardice,
>   Don't count again on me

wrote veteran and poet Louis Simpson, in "Carentan O Carentan."

Once soldiers moved inland, they entered an arena eerily empty of the enemy. Veterans described the battlefield as resembling small groups of men apparently out on a hike, where occasionally one would gesticulate and fall. Contrary to films, where firefights were staged at extremely close range, in World War II high-velocity shoulder weapons distanced the antagonists, riflemen shooting at targets on the far horizon. Opponents manning heavy weapons, such as mortars or artillery, were rarely seen; only the incoming rounds gave notice of their presence. Comrades suddenly getting hit by unseen assailants added to the terror of ground combat.

Battle seemed unreasonable to those engaged, denying to the individual essential knowledge of the factors needed to provide for personal safety. In addition, the senses were confused by noise, chaos, and shocking images of violence. Bullets rained down from a fighter plane that came and went so fast nobody saw it. Unexpected shellfire landed among trucks on a crowded highway, spewing out flesh and twisted metal, preventing movement. The incoming rounds might arrive from the rear, called friendly fire, which fell on its own side far more often than any army was willing to admit. General Mark Clark's boat was nearly sunk by Allied naval gunfire as he went ashore at Anzio, Italy. On July 24, 1944, in a bungled post D-Day operation named "Cobra," U.S. planes twice bombed their own troops. General Leslie McNair died in Normandy from friendly fire. There were thirteen such major errors and countless minor ones from the beaches of France to the Ardennes alone.

If the soldiers saw little, they heard a lot: the sound of both their weapons and the enemy's incoming rounds was deafening. "You don't see much. Mostly you hear it, especially in the jungles. . . . Oh God, your ears ring for hours after," said a veteran of the Pacific theater (Terkel, 376). The men on the ground most feared projectiles that came down from above and against which they had no defense, because you could never burrow into the ground far enough for safety—shells, mortar rounds that descended shrilly from a sheer trajectory, bombs or cannon fire from a strafing aircraft. A dive bomber made you feel your backbone would be laid bare by every concussion.

About 85 percent of physical casualties were caused by shells, bombs, and grenades, only 10 percent or less by bullets. Concussions caused traumatic brain injuries (TBI), physical wounds that produced erratic, disabling behavior. Joe Lanciotti, Sixth Marine Division, wrote after the assault on Sugar Loaf Mountain, Okinawa, that the troops stumbled back down with wounded minds from artillery and mortar blasts that probably would never heal, some of the 26,000 psychiatric cases from Okinawa. Eugene B. Sledge concurred. He thought some marines on Okinawa so stunned by concussion they would live the rest of their lives in mental limbo. As we have only recently started to fully understand the radical mental effects of TBI, it is not surprising that some junior medical practitioners, seeing no apparent physical injuries, accused those suffering internal brain injuries of lacking integrity and dedication. Joe Lanciotti, who was sent for medical observation after he stumbled back down Sugar Loaf, never forgot the young psychiatrist asking him if he was just a coward.

Combat was often characterized by periods of tense expectation punctuated by moments of savage violence. A platoon might be hit by incoming fire, and then suddenly the fighting would wash on somewhere else, leaving the soldiers stunned and bewildered as to what had happened and how. One man might have gone to ground, and there counted the buttons on his jacket; another might have ripped up the earth with his bare hands. Some men had fired their weapons, probably without a target. Others had wept, vomited, defecated in their pants. Someone might have died in panic, like the sergeant who was blown apart when he reached for a grenade in his pants pocket and pulled out only the ring pin, activating the weapon while still on his person. Suddenly, the action stopped. Again unlike the movies, few firefights ended in an acceptable resolution: there was no climax in which a battle was won, a mission accomplished. There was a rain of blind destruction—men were hit, the landscape blasted—then nothing but the moaning. Survivors were left with a disjointed, episodic sense of what had occurred.

Understandably, the mysterious, even incomprehensible, nature of the battlefield provoked intense caution among infantry units. They were reluctant to move forward until artillery and aircraft had plastered the path ahead, imparting a brute force quality to the offensive. Officers and noncoms who pushed on too eagerly, costing lives, were resented and occasionally murdered by their own subordinates. Men who cracked up and became a danger to their own side in battle might be killed through necessity. Veteran Bill Burns recalled that a machine gunner in the Bulge who went mad and could not stop firing his weapon was shot by GIs whose only chance of survival was to surrender to the encircling Tiger tanks.

For many living in 1940s America, domestic conveniences were available to discreetly mask basic animal functions. There were sanitary arrangements for sewage, deodorants to eliminate body odor, vacuums and brushes to sweep away dirt, regular garbage collections, and hygienic and dignified internment for those who passed away. By contrast, the combat soldier was forced daily to witness man as creature, scratching and gouging to live, dying, and decaying. He knew that humans excrete from every pore, that we stink, and in death our bodies become refuse. He lived with perpetual bodily misery. He wore ill-fitting clothes and toted huge burdens. He looked like a hobo. When not under the stress of combat, he endured endless monotony and the fatigue of long marches. He was always tired. One remembered: "My eyeballs burn; my bones ache; and my muscles twitch from exhaustion. Oh, to sleep and never awaken. The war is without beginning, without end. It goes on forever" (Murphy, 46).

The foot soldier rarely got a decent meal; at the front he often went weeks without hot food. Much of his diet was dehydrated: powdered eggs and dried vegetables. He existed endlessly on K rations: spam and dried sausage, crackers and chewing gum. Or C rations: cold stew and candy bars. He needed cigarettes for their warmth and comfort. The front lines reeked of them, along with vomit, for the food soured stomachs. In "The Battle," Louis Simpson, a soldier poet who served in the 101st Airborne Division, wrote: "Most clearly of that battle I remember / The tiredness in eyes, how hands looked thin / Around a cigarette, and the bright ember / Would pulse with all the life there was within."

Men suffered abscessed teeth, stomach ulcers, skin diseases, and other manifestations of malnutrition. Infantrymen were filthy, and many of them said that this was as miserable as being under fire. They had few opportunities to bathe or wash clothes. At least 50 percent of combat soldiers soiled themselves at some time; a last order before battle was, "keep your assholes tight." Men lived in their own filth. Tank crews in action had to defecate and urinate in their vehicles. Troops in foxholes under fire had to foul their positions. They might use a ration can to scoop the waste over the top of the hole. One marine endured constipation for months after his superior officer was shot by a Japanese sniper while exposing himself to enjoy the luxury of squatting for a bowel movement in the open air.

The physical environment became another enemy. In the desert, men suffered from sunstroke, hot winds, and lack of water. There was sand in their food and weapons; its fine grains clogged their vehicle engines, and tank tracks sank in it. In Italy, ground troops struggled against torrential rains, savage rushing rivers, and carefully defended mountain passes with narrow approaches along cliff edges. Throughout the European theater, soldiers confronted severe winter conditions. Snow could be welcomed, as it cushioned shell blasts and could be scooped up to assuage thirst. But intense cold killed the wounded, froze hands, weapons, and feet. Morale became so bad in the winter of 1944–45 that the living said they began to envy the dead.

A Jeep Squashes the Torso of a Dead Enemy. Drawing by Howard Brodie.
Courtesy of the U.S. Army Center of Military History

Marines in the central Pacific fought on bleak, hot, cinderlike coral atolls, which shattered like shrapnel when hit by explosives. To the south, forbidding jungles enveloped troops in claustrophobic dark heat. The lush vegetation played host to a legion of natural dangers, from snakes, insects, leeches, and land crabs to tropical diseases such as malaria, cholera, typhus, and even elephantiasis, which attacked the glands—soldiers' testicles swelled to the size of watermelons. To combat malaria, the troops were given atabrine, which had the side effects of bad taste, nausea, and yellow skin coloration. Many threw the medication away. One 1943 study in the Pacific showed that of 317 fresh wounds, 93 percent showed at least one form of bacterial species, 75 percent had two or more.

Everywhere there was mud. In all theaters, rain turned earth to slime. Men struggled against it in foxholes, where it buried them alive, and drowned in it when shells threw mounds of it upon them. It puckered their skin and rotted their feet. Trench foot accounted for as many as 70 percent of nonbattle casualties during bad weather. When marine Eugene B. Sledge tried to clean up from the fighting on Peleliu, the mud in his hair ripped the teeth from his comb. It had decomposed his socks into slimy webs that pulled the flesh from his feet. Mud acted as a vector for bacteria, such as tetanus and anthrax, that bred in the soil and entered human hosts through cuts and abrasions.

And all around were flies and maggots, for this wasteland of mud and excreta was also a charnel house where the dead lay rotting. In the worst conditions, men ingested insects stuck to their food. Decay accompanied the troops wherever the pace of battle bogged down and bodies could not be removed. On Peleliu, where the opposing lines were so close that it was too dangerous to try reclaiming the dead, bodies oozed into the pervasive slime. Land crabs fed on them.

Stray dogs, hogs, and rats attacked bodies on other fields, such as at Monte Cassino, where they reportedly ate out the tender throats. Insects thrived. An officer stood riveted by the body of a Louisiana boy: "The flies had arrived already and were feasting on the blood in his open mouth" (Gray, 109). The stench from the bodies made eyes run and breathing difficult. Men actually tasted the decay; it made them vomit. Freezing temperatures cut the smell, but then bodies petrified in grotesque contortions of violent death, turning a startling claret color.

Often, there were too many dead for individual burials. On Okinawa, the marines were "stacked like cordwood" awaiting burial in communal graves; so were the Japanese. In Italy, bodies were stuffed in mattress covers and quickly buried. Many corpses were too disintegrated to be reclaimed: vehicles had squashed them into the earth, explosives had blown them apart. At one burial, the only recognizable parts were a scalp and a rib cage. A GI who saw the remains of German panzers caught in Allied crossfire said, "There was nothing," just a pair of boots and "flesh hanging" in the tanks (Decker, 21). Reporter Martha Gellhorn, examining a Sherman tank that had taken a direct hit from a German 88-mm shell, saw only splattered strips of flesh and a lot of blood. Remnants were scraped up and shoveled into holes.

There were 75,000 missing in action (MIAs) in World War II. Most had been blown into vapor when they took a direct hit from heavy munitions. A WAC who assisted families coming to Europe to visit their relatives' graves said: "I don't think they know, in many cases, what remains in that grave. You'd get an arm here, a leg there" (Terkel, 125, 286). An African American member of the quartermaster corps, which dug the graves, said he never got used to the stink. He thought that if every civilian in the world had to smell the rotting corpses, perhaps there would be no more wars.

Only in heroic battle art did the dead assume restful poses, while comrades looked on reverently. Actually, the dead elicited horror. Rifleman Carwood Lipton remembered, "The body doesn't die instantly. The body jerks and snorts and twists, and that shook me up" (Alexander, 111). James Jones said that the living resented the dead for being a messy burden: "Nobody wanted the poor bastard now" (Jones, 159). Violent, unexpected death appeared ugly, embarrassing. It reminded you that, in the scale of things, you were of infinitesimal value, a piece of matter, as bombardier Joseph Heller put it. "Set fire to him and he'll burn. Bury him and he'll rot like other kinds of garbage" (Heller, 450). There was no distinction, said veteran Norman Mailer, between a corpse and a shoulder of lamb.

Often there was little romantic about the way combatants became casualties. William Manchester was wounded by a shell blast blowing parts of his men into his back. A tank officer nearly choked on bone fragments from his shattered left hand. One GI was killed by his buddy's flying head, another by the West Point class ring on his captain's severed finger. A tank rolled over the legs of one horrified boy, already immobilized by wounds. A new phosphorus shell, developed in 1944, threw out pellets that ignited with air to cause massive burns: one member of a forward observer team cracked up when two buddies, hit by friendly fire, spontaneously combusted. The most feared wounds were to the brain, eyes, abdomen, and genitals. Badly wounded men did not always bear their mutilations with stoic patriotism. They felt humiliated and outraged by their predicament; veteran James Jones said they viewed the world with a cold, unforgiving stare. A GI whose arm was blown off in the Arno Valley in Italy cursed both God and America because he suffered "for something I never did or knew anything about" (Fussell, 33).

There was some comfort in the fact that medical discoveries helped the wounded to survive in far higher numbers than in previous wars. Medical advances cut the immediate death rate of wounded at the front from 8 percent in World War I to 4.5 percent in World War II. Four innovations proved vital. Penicillin, produced in quantity by 1943, was a crucial antibiotic, and also pivotal in combating syphilis. Sulfa drugs gave immediate help in preventing wound infection. Medics treated shock, a prime killer in previous wars, through injection of a glucose saline solution, replacing lost blood plasma. But most important were supplies of fresh plasma, reversing the slide into shock.

These emergency measures were administered by medical corpsmen. Casualties were then sent to battalion aid stations, where wounds could be properly dressed. If patients required major treatment, they were transported to portable hospitals, where surgery was performed. These were the MASH units (mobile army surgical hospitals) of World War II. From there soldiers would be sent either to rear hospitals to recover and be returned to active duty or, if incapacitated, evacuated home. Thanks to such sophisticated medical techniques and organization, only one in ten field casualties died, a notable achievement. Unfortunately, some lived on with permanent disability and lasting pain. "The heroes were packaged and sent home in parts," wrote Louis Simpson in "The Heroes." John J. Conroy, a marine shell-shocked and full of shrapnel bits, who had seen most of his buddies killed on Guadalcanal, wrote bitterly, "The medicos here optimistically say I'll pay for it the rest of my life" (Wecter, 545–46).

* * *

Although sailors and airmen normally did not have to endure the filth and char-nel house conditions that ground troops did, their experiences were also harrow-ing. The decks of a fighting ship in action became littered with body parts. One sailor saw his mate blasted through a metal ladder, cutting him into sym-metrical chunks. When a ship sank, many men struggling in the water were dragged down by the undertow. Then, underwater explosions blew them back to the surface, entrails curling from burst stomachs, blood pouring from noses and ears. Men on the surface were coated with oil, which attacked their eyes and lungs. They might or might not be rescued before exposure or sharks claimed their lives.

Airmen in such theaters as Britain and Italy lived comparatively well when not in the air. They had showers, hot food, and recreational facilities. Yet even in Britain, life in temporary buildings, called Nissen huts, was often primitive; crewmen huddled in damp clothing on muddy floors around smoky coal stoves, while wind whistled through cracks in the walls. In zones with intemperate cli-mates and little developed infrastructure, such as Alaska or the central Pacific islands, life could be as stark as for the infantry.

Unlike ground troops, many airmen might be rotated home after a specific number of missions, but this was not always the case. In Alaska, in 1942, there was no rotation for the Eleventh Air Force because there were no replacements. In Europe, a tour was normally twenty-five missions, but during 1943–44, when the air force was waging a war of attrition with the Luftwaffe, the average life of a crew was less than that, at fifteen sorties. Air crews, like other combat troops, cracked up. Occasionally, a pilot went mad in the air and crashed his plane. "There's a point where you just get to be no good; you're shot to the devil—and there's nothing you can do about it," said a naval pilot in the Pacific (Tregaskis, 250). To try to help, crews in some theaters well along in their tour got a week's R and R plus a three-day pass every five missions. But it hardly compensated for what the men went through. Why?

Let's join a bomber crew on a raid over Germany. A mission began with the crew's preparations. These were important. Many airmen were superstitious: they believed their safety depended on dressing in a certain order or carrying a lucky charm. If you got things wrong, your number came up. Next came the briefing and psyching yourself up for combat. Tension mounted. The bombers might wait an hour or more on the runways for the all-clear that led to takeoff. Once air-borne, the flyers were at continual risk. Where the bombers cruised, it was al-ways winter, with temperatures 20° to 50° below zero. The cold was intensified by the bomber's speed, which generated a 150-mph tail wind.

With no insulation or heating, the crew were highly vulnerable. A gunner might lose his fingers if they froze to his weapon. Condensation from oxygen masks dripped down into windpipes and could freeze there, cutting off the oxygen supply: a man might black out and die before he realized the danger. Vomiting into the mask from fear or airsickness provided a similar risk. Usually it was the job of the copilot to check every ten minutes that everyone was all right. Meals for flyers had to be carefully chosen, avoiding foods that caused gas, such as beans, because in the low-pressure atmosphere, pockets of gas in the digestive tract expanded, causing intense pain. Men sometimes had to defecate into their suits to relieve the agony; at other times, their bowels released involuntarily.

The bombers flew in a tight box formation, allowing their machine guns to give maximum mutual protection through an envelope of overlapping fire. A bomber wing or group might throw out thirty tons of steel a minute. But the tight formations also increased the risk of friendly-fire damage and midair crashes, particularly as vapor trails from the engines created a thick haze, through which the planes flew blind. And the silver trails gave away the presence of the bombers to Luftwaffe fighters that, sooner or later, came up to fight.

Combat in the air, as on the ground, was characterized by noise and confusion. With no soundproofing, the racket made by ten or more machine guns clattering at once was almost unbearable. Shell cases flew everywhere. The outside air space became filled with debris and hurtling fighter planes, some of which were your own escort. It was hard to tell the difference. In the mayhem, you might hit one of your own fighters: the gunners' rule was, if it points its nose at you (meaning its guns were brought to bear), you fired.

More feared than the fighter planes was anti aircraft ground fire—shells that burst around you, hurling chunks of flak or shrapnel through the flimsy skin of the bombers. Once the bomber formation locked on target, the planes could not deviate from their flight path. Ground gunners knew this and put up a "box barrage," filling a section of air with flak, through which the bombers must fly. Bert Stiles recalled a shell coming up through the belly of his ship and bursting ten feet above it. A chunk of shrapnel clipped off the pilot's kneecap. Ira Eakin remembered a direct hit on a top gun turret: all that was left of the gunner was his upper teeth stuck in the Plexiglas. Those casualties too severely wounded to make it home were strapped into parachutes and shoved out, in hopes the enemy would hospitalize and not lynch them.

If your ship was crippled, you had to ease out of the formation before parachuting out or risk that you would be pulled into the propellers of the planes behind. One pilot saw a main exit door hurtle past his cockpit, followed moments later "by a man, clasping his knees to his head, revolving like a diver in a triple somersault. I didn't see his 'chute open" (Eckert, 263). A B-17 turned slowly out of formation, its cockpit a mass of flame. The copilot tried to jump from the window and was smashed by backdraft into the tail plane. The plane carrying Lieutenant Murray Greenberg, a navigator with the 8th Air Force, was shot down on February 20, 1944. The pilot bailed out but pinwheeled into the falling bomber, disappearing in a red spray, like a bug on a windshield. If you reached the ground safely, you might still be butchered by irate civilians, frenzied victims of aerial warfare. Pilots in the Pacific freely admitted that they machine-gunned hostile flyers in parachutes, as did the enemy. Much the same was true in Europe, where fighter pilots on both sides routinely strafed enemy flyers who came down in the English Channel.

The planes that survived the outward-bound journey still had to get home, often limping, badly damaged and with gaping holes from flak and fire, one or more props dead, their landing gear collapsed. If you ditched in the sea, you had a 35 percent chance of being rescued before you died from exposure or were machine-gunned from the sky. If you made it home, you had to live with what you had seen and the guilt of knowing you were secretly glad others had died instead of you. Adding to the bizarre nature of the experience, you plunged back into an ordered universe where life might go on almost as though there were no hostilities. If stationed in England, you might go down to the village pub soon after debriefing.

Airmen might feel increasingly distressed by the enormous civilian suffering they inflicted. Alternatively, they could become cynical about the value of human life. War correspondent Ernie Pyle worried about the outlook of young fighter-bomber pilots he met who laughed about how Germans had been blown out of trucks they had shot up, their bodies exploding like firecrackers. Though most bomber crews never had to see close-up the carnage they caused, the dreadful wounds, mutilations, and environmental annihilation, this only partially explains their lack of empathy for civilian victims. Did not these people manufacture the flak and cannon shells that shattered their planes and bodies? Why should they be pitied?

Still, it was the lot of the ground forces to truly experience the full unreason of war's peculiar etiquette about who might be killed and how. For example, it was permissible to slice off an opponent's face with an entrenching tool but not to shoot him with an explosive bullet. You might incinerate him with a flamethrower but not choke him with mustard or chlorine gas. To survive, you sometimes had to do grotesque things that nobody could have warned you about, such as killing an enemy by sticking your fingers in his eye sockets. That some men under stress lost sight of the fine distinctions should not surprise us. What is more remarkable is that most retained their sense of humanity and pulled back from the abyss of savagery.

Inevitably, however, there were crimes and atrocities. For example, before the invasion of Sicily, General Patton told his men to accept no surrender from enemy soldiers who continued to fire within the murderous 200-yard range. At

Biscari, U.S. troops killed thirty-four unarmed prisoners who had given up at the correct distance, but these GIs had seen buddies killed, and they felt a few more yards made no difference. Intelligence officers in all armies admitted that prisoners were tortured, even killed, to extract information. This conduct violated the laws of war, but perpetrators used the same argument advanced to justify dropping the atom bombs: inhumane it might be, but it could save friendly lives. The morality of torture and its efficacy remain controversial. How reliable is information abstracted under extreme duress?

Men in all armies shot prisoners because they were too exhausted to tend to them properly; they had insufficient guards to prevent their captives turning the tables and killing their escorts; or officers said riflemen could not be spared from the line to take prisoners to the rear. For the same reasons, enemy wounded were frequently shot or bayoneted. The perpetrators might be termed murderers, but they were often terminally tired, desperately trying just to survive. Like it or not, prisoners, particularly wounded ones, added to the complexity and hence also the risk of the combat soldier's situation. Many veterans later admitted to taking part in murders, some suffering long-term guilt feelings in the calmer atmosphere of postwar peace.

In Europe, the SS were particularly likely to get no mercy because of their reputation as Hitler's fanatical, cold-blooded killers. The Seventy-Eighth Artillery Battalion of the Second Armored Division called itself "Roosevelt's Butchers" and openly claimed it shot all the SS it caught. In the Pacific theater, toward the end of the fighting, Allied soldiers became hardened to slaughtering Japanese soldiers, since the enemy themselves appeared to have little respect for life. Throughout the war, the Japanese military committed atrocities against captive soldiers and civilians, including the notorious Bataan death march, during which American prisoners were force-marched to death. As the Allies took back territory, Japanese soldiers would often launch hopeless but terrifying suicide attacks against Allied troops rather than surrender. Their ferocity and seeming fanaticism convinced some Western soldiers that only extermination could stop their determination. In the last battles of the war, Japanese soldiers were butchered in enormous numbers. For example, on Okinawa, 7,613 Americans died, but 107,539 Japanese were killed.

Finally, the fighting in the Pacific descended into mutual barbarism impelled by a horrific momentum of hate. Enemy dead were mutilated by both sides. Americans boiled the flesh off Japanese heads and sent the skulls as gifts to loved ones in the States. Ears, hands, and sexual organs were dried for keepsakes. Marines used their large K-bar knives to gouge the gold teeth from dead and dying soldiers, and some admitted that they threw phosphorous grenades into caves sheltering women and children. Garbage was dumped on the enemy dead, and men urinated into their mouths.

These atrocities were symptomatic of war psychosis, a raging anger against the enemy deemed responsible for causing the endless suffering, who must therefore be ruthlessly and utterly subjugated, even to the point of annihilation. This surging ferocity infected every theater of war, particularly the Pacific, but also the Eastern front where Germans and Russians butchered and raped without mercy, and the air war that obliterated Axis cities in response to Hitler's fanatical will to destroy and Japan's refusal to give up. War psychosis must be expected when ordinary human beings are plunged into the extraordinarily violent circumstances of war, there to endure prolonged immersion in its miseries.

CHAPTER FIVE

Home Front Change

In the Great Depression, America's powerful economy seemed to stumble, becoming stagnant. Millions lost their financial investments, millions more were unemployed, and many Americans lost hope of improving their lives. Confidence in liberal capitalism was seriously eroded. The disillusioned turned to socialism, communism, or fascism for alternative answers to the nation's problems. Nazi groups, with names like the Silver Shirts, sprang up across the country, aping the European authoritarian regimes. Though the situation was improving by 1939, the economy remained in low gear. The Roosevelt administration had introduced the New Deal, an unprecedented federal initiative, with agencies dedicated to alleviating unemployment and undertaking public works programs designed to funnel public dollars into national recovery. But Congress was not willing to commit sufficient stimulus funds to get the economy fully back on track. When conflict began in Europe, U.S. unemployment still stood at around 8.9 million.

Wars typically prove a scourge to humanity, increasing the burden of human misery. With Pearl Harbor, the United States was dragged into the maelstrom. Yet here is the remarkable thing. Americans not only came together; domestically the war inaugurated the greatest era of prosperity in human history. The U.S. gross national product increased 60 percent during the war. And while living costs rose 30 percent, total earnings went up 50 percent. By 1945, the United States owned two-thirds of the world's gold reserves, half its shipping, and more than half its manufacturing capacity.

Over time, and as later domestic problems came to seem more intractable, this economic miracle assumed legendary proportions, to a point where anyone who was alive in the 1940s appeared gifted with special powers. World War II and the Great Depression are now nearly as far back as we can go in living memory, and so those events exert a particular fascination, as that era slips from us. Typically, folk history inevitably becomes simplified to make it more accessible. Because of selective recall, we remember mainly that the war not only delivered a huge victory, it also built great national prosperity. The very real achievements of the 1940s have been magnified to appear more spectacular than they actually were. In our collective imagination, not only was America prosperous, but there were no ethnic or gender problems, families were happy and united, and all children worked hard in school and read a great number of books. Americans knew who they were and what was right.

There is a degree of exaggeration in this depiction. To start with, we should observe two major points about the home front boom of World War II. First, the economic recovery of 1940–45 came out of unique circumstances; people erroneously assumed that the boom meant wars would always be good for the whole business community. Second, prosperity, important as it was to Americans' sense of well-being and national identity, did not cure all social problems. Change, even for the better, jolted and disrupted lives. These forceful shifts wrenched and radically altered American society. Also, while the war brought good times for many, it strained family, ethnic, gender, and class relations. Despite the myth that all Americans were well adjusted back then, many felt great anxiety about their society and its future. Let us address these issues separately and in order.

The unemployment left over from the depression was sopped up when 16 million potential workers were absorbed into the military, leaving those at home to take advantage of burgeoning economic opportunities. Perhaps 60 percent of the industrial plant that could be tooled for military production—to make tanks, planes, and so on—lay idle in 1939. Then, huge contracts for arms from Britain and France began kick-starting industrial recovery, shortly aided enormously by America's own demands for military materials. War plants provided many new work opportunities.

Crucially, the government could afford to prime the economic pump because, during the New Deal, the nation's public wealth had not been fully tapped, as it would be now to support the war effort. This ability of government to spend liberally was key to winning the war and domestic economic recovery. The often-voiced idea that the primary agency of economic recovery was private enterprise is misleading; it was, in fact, government spending acting upon an underutilized economy that energized the system. Private enterprise did not have the capital to bankroll a major boom. Had the government spent as much during the depression to pump the economy as it did during the war, it would have achieved the same spectacular results. In the years 1939–41, Congress paid twice as much for defense as it had spent on all New Deal programs in the past eight years. Between 1940 and 1945, the government spent $323 billion, largely on the war effort. Even as early as Pearl Harbor, December 1941, the rate of military spending was $2 billion per month.

Of course, while public spending proved crucial in financing recovery, it was not without long-term costs. Although World War II built American prosperity, this does not mean that the war somehow paid for itself. The immediate cost of the war approximated $381 billion. Only about 44 percent of the bill was paid by direct taxation. The government floated bonds to cover two-fifths of the remainder, then financed the rest through bank loans. The result was that the national debt more than quintupled, from $50 billion to $260 billion, and has not been under that figure since. All of this could be handled in the context of 1945 America because the country was a rich creditor nation with an unprecedented worldwide demand for its goods. Still, it was not until 1970 that the original cost of the war was paid off, and the government continues in the twentieth-first century to be fiscally responsible for pensions and other war-related benefits accrued in the 1940s.

The availability of millions of federal dollars for war contracts inevitably escalated the lobbying activities of large corporations and powerful private individuals eager for a share of the public pie. Their rapacity gave the impression that public favor was for sale and that the relationship between politicians and the privately influential at least verged on the corrupt. Harry Truman, then a senator from Missouri, became appalled by the rapaciousness, greed, fraud, and neglect of vigilance regarding public funds that he felt was overtaking Washington. And Arthur M. Schlesinger Jr., a future distinguished historian and presidential advisor, working in the capital bureaucracy, spoke of greedy corporate CEOs lobbying for preferments while violating price ceilings, and producing shoddy or diluted goods. He concluded, "The home front was not a pretty sight at a time when young Americans were dying around the world" (Schlesinger, 283–84).

It is commonly believed that the war united all Americans in a common cause. As a generalization, this belief has validity: most Americans did support the war effort. But factors in the unstable emergency situation also changed the American way of life in unforeseen ways. As an example, many people today work for large organizations; they often feel small and powerless, lacking control. Dissatisfied, they yearn for a lost golden age they place in the 1940s, a time when small farms and businessmen worked for themselves, an era when, if you built a better mousetrap, the world would beat a path to your door. If such a world existed into the mid-twentieth century, it was in fact undermined by World War II. Many small producers in business and agriculture went to the wall, accelerating the dominance of large corporations that had begun in the Civil War and the Gilded Age. In 1941, there were over 2 million small businesses. Many failed quickly, as products they sold went off the market due to war shortages. Independent car dealers and washing machine distributors provide good examples of little suppliers going under.

In awarding production contracts, the government properly sought the most advanced technology, standardized parts, and economies of scale. This meant that orders went to the big producers, not to small craft shops. America's ten biggest corporations got 33 percent of war contracts. The next largest forty-six companies received a further 42 percent. Not all these giants made arms. Coca-Cola got a massive boost from a contract to supply soft drinks to the forces at a near monopoly. It controlled 95 percent of the overseas PX (post exchange) market, and the government assisted it in adding fifty-four bottling plants to the five existing in 1940. Wrigley's got a boost when its gum was put in GI K-rations. Corporate profits, after taxes, rose by 68 percent during the war.

As the big got bigger, the little were squeezed out. Two months after Pearl Harbor, *Business Week* reported the loss of 200,000 small employers. The growth of big industry led to further radical change. Cities such as Knoxville, Tennessee; Seattle, Washington; and Atlanta, Georgia, all home to war industries, experienced mushrooming growth. In just two years, the Detroit area of Michigan received $11 billion in war contracts. Such cities became host to huge migrant populations. Many migrants were attracted by high factory wages, while others were floating workers from collapsed small businesses and economically depressed towns. Some were farmers displaced by army camps and training ranges, or by the same move in agriculture to large-scale mechanical production methods that changed industry. The new training base at Hinesville, Georgia, for example, threw 15,000 families off the land, while a Procter and Gamble shell-loading facility uprooted 8,000. During the war, number of farms in the United States declined by 17 percent.

Over 15 million civilians moved during the war. To put this in a context, with 17 percent of the population uprooted within a four-year period, this mass migration dwarfed the westward movement of the nineteenth century. From rural Appalachia alone, 700,000 people migrated to cities like Dayton, Ohio; Muncie, Indiana; and Detroit, Michigan. Willow Run, site of a new Ford plant outside Detroit, grew in population from 15,000 to 47,000 almost overnight. Settled inhabitants disliked the incomers, who often had a different cultural style and values. One disgruntled Willow Run native commented: "Everybody knew everybody else and all were happy and contented. Then came that bomber plant and all this influx of riff-raff, mostly Southerners. You can't be sure of these people." A newcomer, equally resentful, said that Detroit was "a city without a heart or a soul" (Winkler, 44).

The inevitable housing shortages led to poor living conditions. By October 1942, in the country as a whole, 1.2 million families were doubled up in one-family units. Basements and garages, trailers, tents, and coal sheds were rented out as homes. Some new homes, quickly built to meet the crisis, had neither water nor sewage lines. By 1945, 5 million families lived in substandard dwellings, such as cellars and woodsheds. Many natives of the mushrooming areas helped the migrant workers, offering free meals to travelers and accommodations at fair prices. Others exploited them. One Connecticut landlord boasted he could rent the same beds to women workers on three separate shifts, so they were occupied around the clock.

Overcrowding became chronic in the neighborhoods allotted to black workers. The population of San Francisco's ghetto doubled, and Chicago's increased by 33 percent. The thrusting together of dissimilar ethnic and regional types generated distrust and hostility. In large areas of the country, segregation in housing, education, and recreational facilities was legal, so when emergency conditions forced working-class whites to live and work with blacks, violence often resulted. In June 1943, prolonged friction between blacks and whites living next door to each other in a predominantly Polish and Irish section of Detroit resulted in race riots. It took 6,000 National Guardsmen to restore order. The costs included thirty-four dead, a million lost work hours, and $2 million in property damage. There were similar riots in New York and elsewhere.

Many plants, such as North American Aviation, would not hire persons of color. In the New Deal era, the federal government had made a Faustian bargain with racist areas of the nation, allowing local agencies to bar blacks from programs. But faced with riots and the threat of civil rights marches on Washington, President Roosevelt established the Fair Employment Practices Committee to investigate hiring abuses. Although it had a small staff and no power to enforce its findings, improvement followed. Where the workplace and worker facilities were integrated, there might be peaceful acceptance of change, but some employers faced white retaliation. White women at a Western Electric plant in Baltimore struck rather than share a restroom with black women.

Pleas to put the war effort first did not always succeed: a white worker in a wildcat strike at a Packard plant said, "I'd rather see Hitler and Hirohito win the war than work beside a nigger on the assembly line." The sociologist Gunnar Myrdal found a majority of whites in the South and West agreed (Tyler, 99). Even faced with such hardline resistance to change, far-sighted African Americans saw factors that could immensely improve their place in society emerging from the booming war economy and the crusade against the nazi superman ideology; they showed a growing interest in advancing civil rights. By 1943, black workers and sympathetic white colleagues began trying to integrate restrooms and eating places, even when served eggshells in their burgers and garbage sandwiches. These pioneers paved the way for the civil rights movement of the postwar era.

Other minority groups also faced continuing prejudice, despite the myth of national unity. Although the Allies opposed Nazis who targeted Jews for liquidation, Jewish American citizens remained victims of discrimination at home. One wartime survey suggested that Caucasians distrusted Jews more than any other minority group, labeling them conniving, greedy, and unpatriotic. They were excluded from country clubs and other social institutions for the elite. Jews in the military, even of commissioned officer rank, experienced serious harassment. As late as December 1944, a poll showed that while most Christian Americans accepted that Hitler had murdered a few Jews, they minimized the scale and enormity of the Holocaust.

Many Hispanics fared badly. As the depression intensified in the early 1930s, fear and anxiety spread among whites that Mexicans and other Hispanics were taking jobs and benefits away from "real Americans." Local, state and national officials launched massive efforts to get rid of Hispanics. Eventually, more than a million Mexicans alone were deported. The removals to Mexico were indiscriminate, as some forced to leave were U.S. citizens. Young Mexican Americans, driven out of their American homeland, entered a cultural no man's land.

As the war neared, American attitudes shifted: deportations slowed, and migrant labor entering the United States from Mexico was encouraged. Youthful Mexican Americans wanted to return to the land of their birth, and Mexican citizens were encouraged to migrate for better wages and job opportunities north of the border, created by labor shortages on the Pacific coast and in the Southwest. However, many workers were still abused and exploited, existing in virtual slavery, forced to work seven-day weeks and stripped of wages to pay for inferior food. Male Mexican Americans, and even Mexican citizens, were drafted, although their parents might be banned from residency in the United States. Many whites still refused to accept the validity of Hispanic immigration, leaving many problems festering into the future.

White uneasiness on the West Coast grew when Mexican American teenagers, like many other adolescents, began forming street gangs and challenging the traditional restraints on their behavior. Identifiable by "zoot suits" (long tapered jackets and baggy pants tied at the ankle, and worn with broad-brimmed hats, an outfit also worn by many young blacks), these youths antagonized white GIs who saw them as flouting the very values they were going off to fight for. (It was

Police arresting Hispanics during the zoot suit riots, June 1943.
Courtesy of the Library of Congress

rumored, incorrectly, that Hispanics were not doing their share in the military.)
In June 1943, the "zoot suit" riots exploded in Los Angeles. For almost a week,
off-duty white enlisted personnel roamed the streets, assaulting Hispanics. When
the police intervened, they often arrested Hispanics, sometimes for their protection. Don McFadden, a sixteen-year-old mechanic, saw servicemen drag a boy
off a trolley and beat him senseless: "Here's a guy riding a streetcar and he gets
beat up 'cause he happens to be a Mexican" (Terkel, 144–45).

Japanese Americans living on the West Coast also became the focus of fear
and hostility after Pearl Harbor. Most of the 47,000 Issei (Japanese born abroad
and therefore banned from citizenship) and 80,000 Nissei (American-born children of the Issei, who were citizens) lived in the Pacific region. They were removed to detention centers in the interior, suffering a $400 million loss in forced
property sales. In a highly questionable 1944 decision, the Supreme Court upheld the legality of the removals. Although most inmates were released later that
year, few received any compensation for the damage done them until the 1980s.

These removals, although intended to prevent Axis subversion, actually hindered the war effort, demoralizing a loyal segment of society and requiring the diversion of military resources to build and guard the camps.

Adding to the strain imposed on housing and transportation facilities by the civilian population movement, millions of service personnel were in transit throughout the war, shifting from one military base to another. Their camps were often bleak facilities, with bars and brothels springing up around them—places soldiers could go to ease their loneliness. There were also cheap souvenir stores selling such items as silver-plated dog tags and china ornaments to send home. Many new military bases were located in the South and West, where legal segregation was standard, on and off base, and black personnel suffered serious harassment. In a Kentucky railroad depot, police beat up three black WACs for using a white restroom. Elsewhere in the state, three women of color in uniform were roughed up and arrested for sitting in the front of a bus.

Northern blacks, unaccustomed to Jim Crow laws, clashed with Southern officials who consigned them to the backs of buses and theaters. Governor Eugene Talmadge of Georgia ordered bus drivers to carry guns and force black GIs to comply with Jim Crow seating. Some white troops supported black soldiers, and the military at times tried to protect its personnel. But the Justice Department was reluctant to challenge local mores: when a black GI was killed by a bus driver in Alexandria, Louisiana, the department would not take up the case. In streetcars, restaurants, and theaters in the South, black soldiers had to sit behind German prisoners of war, who were accorded the rights of white men. Lena Horne, the famous singer, refused to perform in one USO show because German soldiers were seated in front of black GIs, race trumping enemy status.

Service personnel were often followed around the country by their spouses and children. The military proved unsympathetic, seeing women and kids as excess baggage. *Time* reported, on August 30, 1943, that families were the army's last transportation priority, soldiers' dependents often having to stand for whole train journeys or sit on their luggage. The military's hostility extended to denying spouses help in finding jobs to augment their husbands' pay, and refusing to provide army buses to take them to factories. Civilian employers only reluctantly employed army wives, as they quit when their husbands were ordered elsewhere.

Although many townsfolk treated military families well, some cold-shouldered them, resenting the influx of an unstable population. Unused to seeing migrant females in large numbers, some civilians considered army wives "loose" women who "couldn't get enough" and should go back home. Frequently, guest-house owners, fearing for their reputations, prohibited GI husbands from their wives' rooms, so couples met in alleys and phone booths. Housing around camps became overcrowded, and some landlords took advantage of service wives' desperation, jacking up rents and indulging in petty tyrannies, such as banning food and coffeemakers in rooms or neglecting to provide sufficient washing or laundry facilities. In many houses, women had to wait in endless lines to use one cooking stove or bathroom.

Some enterprising landowners put up small sheds to rent out, only big enough to hold one bed, with no amenities. Women with children often could not find lodging at all and had to leave, moving back home with family, experiencing the lack of privacy and independence that had characterized the Great Depression. Women of color had a hard time finding anywhere to rent around bases. At Camp Stewart, Georgia, wives and mothers of black soldiers had to carry army identification papers to keep the local police from arresting them as prostitutes. By contrast, white officers' wives often obtained luxuries like soap in local stores and received prompt dental appointments from off-base practitioners.

This movement of millions of Americans created a breakdown in traditional behavior patterns, leading to growing public anxiety over morality and the integrity of the family. People away from the watchful eyes of relatives and neighbors did indeed violate hometown mores. Data collected from the 1870s on showed that homosexuals were able to meet more freely with others of their persuasion if they lived in cities. Those in rural areas remained isolated and more intimidated by intrusive community attitudes. The vastly increased demographic mobility of World War II, with many more workers migrating to cosmopolitan areas, accelerated this trend to gay urban enclaves, homosexuals finding safety and opportunity in the anonymous crowds of the big cities, using parks, youth hostels, and same-sex bars and clubs to form relationships.

Heterosexuals also found greater sexual freedom. A 1942 survey revealed that only 25 percent of single men and 40 percent of single women abstained sexually. Between 1939 and 1945, the illegitimate birth rate increased 42 percent, to ten per thousand newborns. With couples separated by war, marital fidelity declined, and the divorce rate rose—from 16 percent in 1940 to 27 percent in 1944. By then, 3 million marriages had broken up under the strain of wartime absences.

A joint government and business campaign to get married women to do paid work added to the stress on traditional marriages, challenging the conventional wisdom that a wife should be a full-time homemaker. By 1942, the white male unemployment pool had largely dried up, and new worker groups were needed. Married white women became the most obvious labor source, and so propaganda badgered and enticed them into the labor market. "Mrs. Stay-at-Home" was the target of ads saying that women were not doing their share. A 1943 editorial in the *Baltimore News Post* told unemployed wives: "Sister you'd better reform"

(Anderson, 28). The War Manpower Commission asserted that "women have been allowed to fall into habits of extraordinary leisure" and were "getting by just by being 'a good wife and mother'" (Rupp, 97).

Women were also told that they had overprotected their children and that "momism" had spoiled male adolescents, accounting for high failure rates among army inductees to reach basic physical and mental toughness standards. The upshot was an influx of married women into the job market. In 1944, for the first time, married female workers outnumbered single female workers, representing 72 percent of the increase in employed women since 1940. By then, 19 million women had paid jobs. However, we should not exaggerate the extent of real change this represented: despite the Rosie the Riveter image, two-thirds of adult females remained full-time homemakers. Moreover, 11.5 million of those in jobs had worked in 1940. And for only a handful of women was this their first job; most had worked before marriage. Nevertheless, serious change affecting the lives of many families was real enough.

By no means everyone supported women being war workers. Conservative journals such as *American Home* and the Catholic *Commonweal* urged wives to stay home. A judge in Seattle ordered a woman to quit working when her husband threatened divorce. Many Americans thought that married female factory workers were immoral and assumed that extramarital sex was common on the night shift, a claim that some surveys seemed to bear out. Male workers exhibited open hostility to women applying for the same work they did.

Many women felt great guilt about appearing to shirk their family responsibilities and tried to do two jobs, one in and one out of the home. They got some help from day-care centers for infants, but these were mainly of two kinds: expensive preschools for the rich and charitable institutions for the poor. The middle class got largely cut out of the picture. The Works Progress Administration, a vestige of the New Deal, had 1,500 nurseries to help the very poor, but the WPA was abolished in 1943 and the nurseries went with it. The few day-care establishments available to the middle class were often inconvenient to get to, and their use carried a stigma of parental neglect, so most women relied on family help with children instead and worked hard to accommodate both home and employer.

Working outside the house and looking after a family grew exhausting. By 1943, a third of female war workers also had children at home. And looking after a house was harder then, as fewer convenience foods and labor-saving devices existed. Also, with the rationing of food and other household items, women had to spend more time shopping than previously. Women who worked nights might get home at 7:30 a.m. After a short sleep, they would get up to shop, clean, wash clothes, and cook for husbands and children. One working woman rose at 5:45 a.m. to cook the family breakfast before punching in at work at 7 o'clock. Some nights, if she did not manage to put dinner on the table by 6 o'clock, her husband got angry. Food stores, asked to make a minimal accommodation, stayed open one night a week to enable female workers to shop.

Ironically, although housewives were the group most affected by shortages of staple goods, prejudice against seeing women as policy makers meant that they were largely excluded from service on war rationing boards. A committee established to advise the War Food Administration on nutritional needs was composed entirely of male physicians. Not one home economist or dietician (fields staffed by women), who might be presumed to know at least as much about diet as physicians, was appointed to the group.

By 1944, as the conflict progressed and the need for war workers wound down, public opinion about the need for women in paid employment shifted to the negative. In part, this shift reflected a growing unease about children being neglected. (Many females, overworked to exhaustion, wished to drop out of the job market anyway: by early 1944, the strain on working women produced high absenteeism and labor turnover.) Media pundits, the fickle arbiters of public opinion, having stoked public anxiety about "momism," now reversed course and belabored women for neglecting their children by taking paid employment: "eight-hour orphans" and "trailer park toddlers" became common terms to rebuke working mothers.

Of most concern to social critics was the seeming increase in emotional and behavior problems among adolescents, particularly those left for long periods without adult supervision. The depression appeared to have weakened parental authority. The 1930s witnessed fathers' stature diminished by unemployment or reduced wages, undercutting their role as breadwinners and voices of authority in the family. Geoffrey Gorer, a visiting English academic, observed that, in a row over who should use the family car, dads usually lost out to kids.

After 1941, fathers and elder brothers often were away at war, so important role models were lost. If the mother worked, too, the stage seemed set for wildness among unsupervised children of both sexes. Adults worried about adolescent hostility and rebellion, expressed in growing numbers of street gangs. Cutting school increased: in Detroit, truancy jumped 24 percent between 1938 and 1943. More girls got pregnant. And the venereal disease rate rose: between 1941 and 1944, New York city's VD rate among girls aged fifteen to eighteen increased 204 percent.

Delinquency came out of a larger trend: the birth of teen culture as a separate and distinct phase of American life. Many aspects of adolescent group behavior that concern social critics today were already becoming apparent in youth of the 1940s. Other factors were at play in this development besides the weakening of family ties through parental absenteeism. To begin with, there appeared to be a decline in the authority of schools and the intellectual quality of education. The denunciations of the teaching profession at the time make clear that upholding educational standards proved difficult in wartime. But even before the war, in the 1930s, unease developed about shifting trends in pedagogy.

Standardized tests, used to cope with large class numbers, were accused of producing a drop in analytical and writing skills. Many lessons and examinations looked like checklists of unrelated facts and dates with little relevance to a given body of knowledge. Civics, for example, often meant not much more than rote learning the Bill of Rights, with little explanation of the document's relevance to students' lives. The bar for passing from one grade to the next appeared to be dropping. Army recruiters found inductees poorly prepared in the hard sciences and foreign languages.

Mass entertainment competed with books for youth's attention, as students devoured film, radio, and comic books. Philip Wylie, a social critic, said that youth could no longer speak or write properly. It was estimated that by 1941 most teens listened to two to three hours of pop music per night. Adolescent devotion to singers such as Frank Sinatra worried adults who saw teenage girls mob him in the streets and swoon in pseudosexual ecstasy at his concerts. One reporter said that Sinatra "generated the nearest thing to mass hysteria in the country" (Gervasi, 440). A pervasive anti-intellectualism characterized many students: school heroes were athletes, while literature, music, and art courses got tagged as boring, irrelevant to "real life."

Of course, the roots of many problems went back further than the war, to methods of learning that emphasized rote memorization over intellectual curiosity, producing many adults with poor analytical skills. As an example, on Halloween eve in 1938, Orson Welles produced a radio play based on English author H. G. Wells's 1897 science-fiction thriller, *The War of the Worlds*. Although the program gave clear pointers that it was purely drama, not on-the-spot journalistic reporting, communities across America exhibited mass hysteria, people fleeing their homes and swamping police dispatchers with pleas for protection. One widespread rumor said Martians had invaded, another that the Germans had taken New Jersey. The embarrassing episode suggested a widespread inability in adults to filter data rationally rather than make gut responses.

Nevertheless, whatever earlier intellectual failings paved the ground, the war years exacerbated educational problems. The draft caused a drop in the quality of secondary teachers, yet Congress in 1943 killed a bill to raise teachers' pay and so attract better faculty. In urban areas swamped by population influxes, schools had to go on split sessions, and their facilities were run down by overuse. The draft had another direct impact on secondary and higher education: to speed boys through to induction, schools and colleges cut the requirements for graduation. And the needs of the army and navy also caused universities to offer fewer liberal arts courses and more technical and vocational subjects. Military development projects, funded by federal grants, moved the focus from pure to applied scientific research and forged a link between university research and defense programs that continued after the war.

Campuses became host to military training units. By 1942, Harvard had 4,500 troops training on its campus; the president of the University of California at Berkeley described his school as approximating a circus, with a big military tent and academic sideshows. A 1943 report by the American Association of University Professors, the watchdog society for higher education, warned that the needs of the military were not only dictating curriculum but also forcing the hiring of airplane mechanics and other technicians as teachers, staff who would normally be located in vocational schools. The report also alleged that universities were using the emergency as an excuse to fire professors with unpopular views, eroding academic freedom in the name of patriotism.

Even before the war, minimalism frequently characterized the level of debate in secondary schools about public issues. World history and current events had often been poorly covered by educators, so that most students had little or no understanding of Asian issues and not a clue as to why Japan attacked us in December 1941. The wartime teaching of social studies proved no better: a 1942 poll showed that 44 percent of high schoolers could not say what the war was about. Some actively resented the space it took up on the radio and in magazines. A typical world history text of 1943 devoted 2.7 percent of its pages to China and Japan and 1.6 percent to East Asia. Hawkish citizens' groups forced the revision of social studies texts to expunge any comments critical of past U.S. policies and practices, on the basis that these promoted disunity in a time of national crisis. For example, negative comments on slavery or treatment of Native Americans had to be eliminated.

However, the shortcomings of neither parents nor educators were primarily responsible for the major characteristics of teen culture. The war's most serious impact on youthful behavior was through prosperity and enhanced job opportunities, generating immense spending power that spawned all-important consumer rituals and peer pressure to be up on the latest fashions. This affluence, more than anything else, skewed the high school from a seat of learning into a social center, the fulcrum of teen life, where study competed with athletics, hair styles, clothing, pop idols, and dates. In this closed world, peer approval loomed omnipotent, and adult concerns increasingly remote.

With many youthful adult males in the armed forces, jobs not usually available to younger teenagers, such as bowling alley attendants, opened up. Whole new work areas arose, including babysitting needed by women workers. Many employers found they liked hiring adolescents because they were more pliable than adults and worked cheaply. The result was that teens entered the work force in larger numbers than any other group. From 1940 to 1943, the number of working teens rose 300 percent. By 1942, 3 million youngsters aged fourteen to seventeen had jobs.

Much teen work was not essential to the war effort, yet schools felt obliged to modify their schedules to meet the demands of working students and their employers. The state superintendent of public instruction for Indiana urged schools to hold paid student working hours to four per day, but he also told principals to allow more if employers demanded it. Some schools consented to a fifty-fifty split between work and school. Many closed down altogether during peak consumer periods, such as Christmas rush. In a sense, school authorities felt trapped into compliance because failure to acquiesce meant students dropped out. One state experienced a 17 percent increase in dropouts between 1940 and 1944. Schools increasingly gave credit for outside work and yielded to student demand for vocational courses useful in the marketplace. The upshot was that some education became intellectually shallow and vocation-oriented.

The resultant adolescent affluence, more than any other factor, lay at the root of the new teen culture, a potent innovation in American life. While the Great Depression had extended adulthood downward, thrusting grown-up status and problems on children at an early age, wartime affluence extended childhood upward, creating adolescents who often lacked maturity and direction. By 1944, teens were estimated to have a purchasing power of $750 million and, as adults bought the necessities, this money was virtually all discretionary income, to be spent on amusements. The media and business quickly exploited this affluence with products often frivolous and overpriced. New magazines, such as *Seventeen*, *Young America*, and *Calling All Girls*, tapped the juvenile market. Fads, such as wearing jewelry decorated with the American flag, sold to students as a contribution to the war effort, swept the schools; epidemic buying became a feature of juvenile life.

Many adults, who felt that the depression had robbed them of their innocence, smiled on this youth culture. But seeming adolescent immaturity and disrespect for age also provoked bewilderment and unease. Teens' freedom seemed to symbolize, painfully, a world in flux, a world less and less subject to control by adults. Money meant freedom, since juveniles could afford the gas and cars to get out from under their parents' supervision. Polls showed that teens thought gas rationing the worst privation of the war. With their new wealth and independence, kids threw drinking parties and stayed up all night smoking cigarettes and reefers (a combination of tobacco and marijuana) in cinemas and bowling alleys. A rash of vandalism erupted, such as slashing seats on public transport and stealing cars to joyride. The delinquency rate in Detroit increased 24 percent between

1938 and 1943. Of most concern to the white middle class, the rise in crime rate for white youth outpaced that for blacks by 250 percent.

What was happening? Studies suggested that business prosperity and juvenile delinquency moved in the same direction. Money gave young people an exhilarating sense of unrestricted freedom and unaccustomed power, producing immature or wild behavior. One irate letter to the *Indianapolis News* said that youth had too much, was coddled, and had too few demands placed on it. "They must have thrills, speed, excitement; that's one reason why they break laws" (Ugland, 261). The visiting French aviator and writer Antoine de Saint-Exupéry, author of *The Little Prince*, said being a consumer gave life no purpose: American young, bored and at loose ends, often seemed ripe for problems.

The ultimate difficulty was that, prosperous and unfettered as they might be, juveniles were peripheral to the great events taking place. They were marginal to the war effort and often felt undervalued. Adolescents embraced individual freedoms and yet felt excluded from the larger world. Some teachers and civic officials understood this and enlisted young people in the war effort through such activities as collecting scrap metal for the arms industry or building model planes for use in the military's aircraft spotting exercises. But some activities were of little importance, even silly at times, as when whole schools wore the national colors to "encourage" the troops. The frustration of feeling small and foolish provoked delinquency, frustrated teens antagonizing adults to get their attention.

Boys could aspire to be soldiers when they reached enlistment age, but girls had few outlets for their patriotism. Many were too young to be USO workers, dispensing refreshments and entertainment to soldiers. They could write to a man overseas, but this was remote from daily reality—so girls who would not have sex with a civilian willingly gave themselves to men in uniform. It was estimated that 85 percent of the girls near army bases who had frequent sex with soldiers were not prostitutes but amateurs who did not charge. Camp commanders had to deal with irate parents of teenage girls pregnant with illegitimate children, intent on hunting down the fathers. Requests for social services for unwed mothers more than doubled in the first two years of war.

These adolescents trying to do their bit were called Victory Girls. Many came out of their war experience all right, but others experienced severe psychological repercussions. One Victory Girl was fourteen and playing with dolls on the day Pearl Harbor was bombed. She never played again: her father went away to do war work, and her mother was too busy watching over a large family to notice each child individually. She soon went off with uniformed men, sometimes two or three a day. This fed her young ego but also made her wild. She developed a local reputation for being fast and was shunned by family and neighbors. After so many brief liaisons in her formative years, she had trouble later forming stable relationships. After the war, she had three marriages, all failures. Looking back in 1985, she felt that the war had given her too much adult freedom too quickly.

Young people who reached puberty in the late 1940s and early 1950s did not know that the teen culture they inherited was less than a decade old; they took it as a birthright. The hallmarks of this culture included lack of personal responsibility, broad freedoms enjoyed in separation from the larger, mature society, and a pervasive anti-intellectualism. An Italian American, looking back on the war, most regretted that it led his generation to pursue shallow excitements sold by the commercial leisure industry, rejecting the cultural traditions of their ethnic communities. In particular, Italian American youth no longer cared for opera, which in his youth had enriched ordinary Italian Americans' daily lives but now only highbrows and eggheads appreciated.

At one level, some teen behavior merely aped adult patterns. Older people might call juveniles frivolous and irresponsible, but many grown-ups also enjoyed accelerated buying power and shared little of the sacrifice of Americans overseas. Lee Oremont, a supermarket owner in Los Angeles, whose business did very well serving war workers, recalled: "I think the war was an unreal period for us here at home. Those of us who lost nobody at the front had a pretty good time. The war was not really in our consciousness as a war" (Terkel, 313–14). Those who visited the hospitals, such as the popular singing group, the Andrews Sisters, saw some of the war's human cost. "We saw boys with no arms or legs, with half-faces." But they too did very well out of the war, and it was hard not to enjoy it—their audiences were large, and their records were big sellers. Maxene Andrews recalled: "There was a sort of frenzy and a wonderful kind of gaiety. There was much more money around than there had ever been" (Terkel, 292).

Many people rationalized doing well from the war because they were involved in war work or other essential labor and could therefore say that their affluence was a fruit of patriotism. One woman who made and spent a lot of money during the war said, "It had been an enjoyable experience. . . . I was glad I did it, that I'd done my part" (Gluck, 113). Her association of fun and duty was not cynical. For many civilians on the "production front," the war allowed a correlation between victory and self-interest. A lot of people did their best to conserve, live frugally, and put their spare earnings into war bonds. But it was also true that corporations, organized labor, and many individuals equated their own interests with the national good, rationalizing self-indulgence as patriotism: victory, they asserted, would come substantially through Americans making and spending on the home front.

Business attacked labor organizers, suggesting that worker agitation caused loss of productivity and led to the deaths of soldiers. But business, too, exploited the conflict. As Theodore S. Repplier, executive director of the Advertising Council, put it: "Business and advertising have a continuing social responsibility, *which brings rich returns to those who act on it*" (Fox, 55). Business got immense tax incentives because, as Secretary of War Henry L. Stimson said, corporations would not fully cooperate otherwise. In return for being on the team, big business also insisted that New Deal social welfare programs be curtailed, stunting their development at a crucial stage.

The legislation introducing Social Security in 1935 faced significant opposition, preventing it from accomplishing universal old-age pension coverage. Many workers, particularly in rural areas, especially the South, were excluded from the scheme. Benefits were low and could not be drawn upon until five years after entering the program. Many employees resented paycheck deductions, begun in 1937, and companies protested paying Social Security taxes. Corporations took advantage of wartime prosperity to offer alternative pension schemes, insinuating that a public program was superfluous and constituted a government invasion of private and individual rights. In 1940–45, 2.25 million employees gained private pensions, and obtaining such a benefit package became part of the American dream. Over the long term, this meant that the federal Social Security program remained controversial, failing to gain acceptance as a universal welfare benefit and so not covering all workers while increasingly demonized as an illegitimate "entitlement."

Much the same happened with the New Deal attempt to provide national health care coverage as a right of citizenship. By the 1930s, rising health care costs accounted annually for an average 5.2 percent of family expenses. The availability of medical attention varied widely across the nation. New Deal administrators made public health care a significant part of planning for broad relief and economic recovery efforts. For example, the Federal Emergency Relief Administration provided group medical care for the poorest farmers, while the Works Progress Administration and the Public Works Administration funded new public sanitation and hospital projects. When these programs ended in the war, so did their medical relief efforts.

Despite the need for further reform to ensure all Americans received basic medical coverage, the American Medical Association and conservative politicians fought federal involvement in the distribution of health care as socialism, effectively curtailing public discussion. The military took care of the medical needs of millions. And corporations, facing government caps on wages, offered private medical insurance as an employment incentive. As a result, the private medical insurance industry assumed giant proportions, while overall American health care remained a cobbled-together patchwork, leaving outside of the medical safety net millions of inner city and rural poor, employees of small businesses, along with patients suffering from preexisting conditions. As late as 1945, a Senate committee found that 40 percent of U.S. cities lacked sufficient qualified physicians and adequate hospital facilities.

Despite posing as disinterested patriots, company executives openly exploited the war to popularize their brands. General Electric touted a Mazda light bulb "that survived Pearl Harbor." Radio commercials for funeral homes and burial plots always aired when the casualty lists were disclosed. One ad suggested that to the Four Freedoms should be added a fifth: freedom from ruptured hernias through using their trusses. "You're unpatriotic, That's what!" was the cry of a husband whose shrunken shirt proved that his wife had failed to buy a Sanforized brand (Fox, 34, 37).

Business diminished the ideological meaning of the struggle between totalitarianism and democracy, equating freedom with consumer choice. Prevented after 1942 from making such items as cars, refrigerators, and toasters, business identified the Axis as enemies primarily of free enterprise and defined victory as the renewal of consumer choice. "WHAT THIS WAR IS ALL ABOUT," said one Royal typewriter ad, was the right to "once more walk into any store in the land and buy anything you want." The *New York Daily News* said the war was being fought to return to baseball and a full tank of gas.

Organized labor sometimes showed the same narrowness of vision. Industrial strikes doubled between 1942 and 1943 and jumped again in 1944 to 1945. In 1944 alone, nearly 9 million workdays were lost to strikes. That same year, as Allied victory seemed assured, absenteeism became chronic, and voluntary labor turnover (workers quitting) reached 61 percent in the manufacturing industries. Much of this was due to stress on workers, including pressure on women to return home and raise the kids. But much came sheerly from the search for higher wages and better positions at the expense of war production.

People in the 1940s were no more and no less dedicated and selfless than other generations. John Kenneth Galbraith, an economist put in charge of price controls in 1942, recalled that in the war years domestic consumption doubled. "Never in the history of human conflict has there been so much talk of sacrifice and so little sacrifice," he quipped (Terkel, 320). Many businessmen and consumers had come to equate democracy less with the right to vote than with the right to shop. Military victory might be the means, but consumption was the end. Perhaps after the deprivation of the depression, this could be expected.

The taste for goods was sharpened by a combination of shortages and high wages. In addition to the ban on mechanical items such as radios, record players, and vacuum cleaners, staples like butter, sugar, and gas were rationed. Even women's stockings were in short supply. As items became scarce in 1942, panic buying ensued; customers stampeded meat markets and hoarded essentials, adding to the general scarcity. A black market developed, patronized by people who saw themselves as 100 percent American; middle-class customers and their regular merchants colluded to cheat fair rationing. One-third of those questioned by pollsters admitted that they would buy anything they needed on the black market.

Many Americans, for the first time in history, had more money than they knew what to do with. The gap between the top fifth and bottom fifth in income actually narrowed for the only time in the century. The middle class made the greatest proportionate gain. A lot of people had discretionary income, and business shaped new spending habits to tap this wealth. Some consumers would buy anything. Tiffany's sold a $5,000 V for Victory brooch. One store manager said, "People want to spend money, and if they don't spend it on textiles they'll spend it on furniture; or . . . we'll find something else for them." The average department store purchase rose from two dollars to ten dollars during the war (Winkler, 34).

With many families enjoying two incomes, what constituted need was reassessed, beginning a trend to making many luxuries into necessities. The war created a new and materialistic middle class. In 1944 the shops were stripped of goods long before Christmas, and on December 7, the anniversary of Pearl Harbor, Macy's had its best sales day ever.

However, if prosperity grew on the home front, an air of anxiety remained, and may have actually intensified as the war neared its end. One major fear was that there would be a new and worse depression when millions of men in uniform were demobilized, flooding the job market at the very time when war industries would be retooling for peacetime production.

Just as disturbing for America's stability was that perceived decline in family values. "Are we facing a moral breakdown?" was by 1945 a favorite radio talk show topic. Delinquency continued to rise, as did divorce, with half a million breakups in 1945. Many failed relationships came out of unique wartime circumstances: young women had felt moral pressure to marry a GI and send him overseas happy. Often such whirlwind romances, fueled by the adrenaline flow of war, could not survive sustained separation or the reality of daily contact in the flatter atmosphere of peace. Where couples demonstrated clear incompatibility, war marriages were best ended. But critics also saw in the statistics a decline in American values and identified women working outside the home as the major culprit. A 1945 State Farm Insurance ad showed a hysterical girl being carted away to a foster home because her mother was out working. Women were urged to leave their positions, making slots available for returning veterans and restoring female focus on building a healthy home environment.

"Mother, When Will You Stay Home Again?" Advertisement for Adel Precision Products Corp.
Saturday Evening Post, May 1944. Used courtesy of Imo Industries Inc.

There was gratitude to women for their contribution to the war effort, but this stopped short of according them full legal equality. In 1945, the Equal Rights Amendment failed in the U.S. Senate. As the war ended, a disproportionate number of women workers were laid off. Many accepted this cheerfully, but others felt betrayed by the turnaround. A fired woman worker at the Tacoma Navy Yard said that many women like her were angry about their redundancy, having tasted the benefits of income independence.

The exodus of women from the work force is intelligible when we understand that the bulk of Americans of both genders had seen women's war work as temporary and not a permanent change in labor patterns. Throughout the war, ads reminded women that despite working, their first priority remained looking attractive to men. The *Detroit News*, for example, suggested that the ideal female riveter was a cross between a beauty queen and a Hollywood starlet. A Tangee lipstick promotion said that one reason America was fighting was for the precious right of women to return to being feminine and lovely (meaning ornamental). The continuing accent on sex appeal suggests how little real change the war had inaugurated in the acceptable female persona. Despite the showcasing of wartime working women, they had not really broken through the major barriers keeping the professional world a white male preserve.

Men abandoned certain areas of work as women joined the work force in 1942. Clerical, typing, and secretarial jobs, split fifty-fifty between the sexes in 1940, constituted a female domain by 1945. Bank tellers and store clerks also came to be primarily female positions. The ranks of traditionally female occupations, such as nursing and teaching, swelled with new recruits, But women remained underrepresented in advanced technical work, like chemical and electrical engineering. They gained little ground in law or medicine and were kept out of most supervisory positions in business and industry, the assumption being both that their careers were temporary and that they were temperamentally best suited to low-level, repetitive work. Further, they earned 60 percent of the male rate for the same work.

A majority of middle-class women who could afford to quit working after the war wanted to. One postwar poll showed that 76 percent of returning homemakers felt they had made no sacrifice in quitting. After all, much wartime employment for women was unattractive, characterized by long hours and tedious and repetitive tasks in dirty, unhealthy surroundings. In 1946, seven of eight adults polled felt that homemaking constituted a full-time job. The revolution many women of this generation wanted was not in the marketplace but the home. They wished to return to the kitchen but not to re-create the world of their mothers; they would reinterpret it.

A dominant memory was of the depression and extended families: parents, siblings, grandparent, aunts, and unemployed uncles living on top of each other in cramped old houses, with little privacy or room for individuality. Parents had controlled the behavior and finances of unmarried daughters, whose wages went into the family kitty. These daughters, now grown, dreamed of new, clean, well-lit, one-family homes in the suburbs, where they would have the latest labor-saving devices and could raise a nuclear family with the privileges and luxuries lacking in their youth. This was their dream of independence. For many women, war work interrupted their hopes, even if the prosperity of wartime meant that their aspirations could be fully realized after the war.

The Rosie the Riveter image should not obscure the fact that the major enhancement of women's role in the war was not as producer but consumer of goods. Women, along with juveniles, became the major buyers, particularly as traditionally male items, such as cars and lawn mowers, were off the market. And the role of consumer fit perfectly with middle-class female yearnings for suburbia. From 1944 on, women's magazines, powerful organs of consumerism, shaped and supported this vision, carrying major articles on the new "victory home" and the wonderful world of appliances shortly to be available to the homemaker. Thus, the war did not inaugurate the radical feminist campaign: that came later, in the late 1960s and 1970s, as a reaction to the role of suburban housewife by daughters of the women who had embraced it in 1945 and 1946.

Overall, the war brought great prosperity to the United States, with many Americans, though not all, sharing in it. But it also brought great geographic and social changes. The strain in the cultural fabric elicited a conservative reaction by 1944, leaving America rich but facing the postwar world with an undercurrent of popular anxiety.

CHAPTER SIX

The World Created by War

Throughout World War II, both sides spoke of bringing a new world order to bear through the triumph of their values. Promises of finer days ahead became part of the compensation governments offered for their citizens' suffering and sacrifice. In August 1941, the United States and Britain declared that they were dedicated to the principle of national self-determination and to Four Freedoms: freedom of speech and religion, freedom from want and fear. By January 1, 1942, twenty-six Allied nations had endorsed these goals. With the 1945 unconditional surrender of the major Axis powers, an era of peaceful international cooperation and coexistence might be anticipated.

At home, despite a short-lived economic depression immediately after the war, America grew more prosperous than before the conflict. During the war, about 64 percent of Americans had become homeowners, versus 44 percent on the eve of war. Many new products enhanced the quality of life, from antibiotics in medicine to home aids like automatic washers and dryers, first marketed in 1946. These were good times, and Americans could take pride in their achievements, both at home and abroad. It was not unreasonable to think that the future would be calm, comfortable, carefree.

Secretary of War Henry L. Stimson captured the spirit of growing optimism during the struggle, saying in the introduction to *Prelude to War* (1942), a film in the Why We Fight series: "We are determined that before the sun sets on this terrible struggle our flag will be recognized throughout the world, as a symbol of freedom on the one hand . . . and of overwhelming power on the other." Unfortunately, this picture of unity and amity at home and abroad was to some degree misleading. Wartime propaganda had pasted over divisions between the major Allied nations and ignored crucial divisions on the home front that would not go away. Many veterans and civilians would have trouble adjusting to their new circumstances. Americans would clash over race relations; eventually America's cities would burn and civil rights champions would die. The fragile alliance with Soviet Russia would shortly distort into the Cold War, and the Chinese nationalists would lose control of the mainland to the communists.

In 1945, when it became clear that the Soviets would not support the principle of national self-determination in their sphere, the United States, with its dominant economic and political power, stepped forward as the leader of the free world, indirectly confronting the Soviets through proxy wars and competition for allies. Over the long term, American wealth would be siphoned off increasingly into bolstering that "overwhelming power" Secretary Stimson had talked about. When he retired from the presidency in 1960, distinguished former army general Dwight D. Eisenhower warned of an emerging military-industrial complex coming to dominate the U.S. economy and life. By that time, the United States and the Soviet Union were the major arms suppliers to the world, a trend begun in the war, and one that encouraged small conflicts around the globe. The Cold War would entail compromising American values. And over everything hung the specter of nuclear war, haunting succeeding generations.

Let us look first at the international picture. World War II could not create a world free from conflict because there was never a realistic possibility that the democracies and the Soviets would form a lasting partnership or that the communists would move after the war to a more representative form of government. For most of communist Russia's existence there had been hostility with the Western democracies. When America and Russia became allies, in December 1941, some hoped this forced marriage would lead to better understanding and cooperation for world peace. To encourage acceptance of Russia as an ally, wartime propaganda, particularly film, played down Soviet authoritarianism, picturing the Russians as hard-working, down-to-earth people, akin to Midwesterners. In a world divided by the media into Axis slave powers and Allied free nations, the Russians had to be portrayed this way. Polls showed a majority of Americans in 1942–44 saw the Russians, rather than the British, as most like themselves, demonstrating the power of the media to change an image quickly. *Time* magazine named Josef Stalin 1943 "man of the year."

At the highest political level, President Franklin D. Roosevelt developed a viable working relationship with Stalin, as he did with Winston Churchill. Both FDR and Stalin believed in the crucial role of great powers, and neither intended their nation's policies to be dictated after the war by smaller states. Roosevelt framed his concept of a United Nations so that major powers—America, Russia, Britain, and China—would dominate through the Security Council and, through individual veto power, retain complete autonomy. Each power would have a regional sphere of influence and act as the world's policeman within it, thus guaranteeing peace. FDR hoped that bringing Russia into a leadership role in the family of nations would develop a greater sense of security among the Soviet leadership and, consequently, a liberalization of the communist system.

Realistically, such a scenario was unlikely. The success of FDR's plan rested on his personal relations with other world leaders, but since Stalin did not respect the principle of national self-determination or the Four Freedoms, the ultimate scenario could not be realized. From late in the war, Soviet brutality in Eastern Europe made the American media stop its positive portrayal of Russians. "Do you know what it was like to be a woman when the Russians came in?" asked Marlene Dietrich in *A Foreign Affair* (1948), playing a Berliner who had been raped by the Russians. Rape now seemed a fitting symbol for Russia's foreign policy.

During the war, relations between the United States and Soviet Union had already soured at the highest military levels through different perceptions of the load each was carrying. The Russians, who bore the brunt of the German ground onslaught from 1941 on, argued that the Western Allies failed to do their share before the D-Day invasion of June 1944. While the British and Americans faced twelve Axis divisions in Italy, the Soviets were fighting 180 divisions on the eastern front. But the democracies responded that they also had to fight the Japanese and could not realistically invade Hitler's Fortress Europe until their navies won the battle of the Atlantic and their war planes controlled the air space over Western Europe.

The Russians also questioned the British-American demand for Germany's unconditional surrender. They suspected that this was intended to rob the Nazis of hope and make them fight to the last ditch, consequently butchering more Russians. In fact, the democracies' major concern was avoiding a repetition of 1918 when Germany had been allowed to surrender before the complete defeat of its armies, a fact that led Hitler to argue Germany was not defeated by enemies but betrayed by its liberal politicians. This time the Nazis would fight to the death. The United States and Britain sent lend-lease military aid to Russia, which helped relations, but according to insiders like Charles Bohlen of the State Department, the United States sometimes promised more than it could deliver. And late in the war, Joe Marcus, an administration official, said the United States reneged on shipments of war matériel for fear they would be used against American forces in a future confrontation. The allegation had some basis.

Two issues were ultimately crucial to the lasting estrangement between Russia and the United States. The first was spheres of influence. By 1939, Stalin believed that a great nation's security lay in having smaller puppet states along its borders to offer a buffer zone against invasion. The war furthered his belief. Twice in thirty years Germany attacked Russia through eastern Europe. The Soviets craved territorial security at any price. But Russia's preoccupation with a buffer zone of subject states meant the blighting of democratic hopes for countries caught in the Russian sphere at the end of war, alienating America and Britain.

The second major area of contention was over nuclear weapons: the democracies did not trust the Russians sufficiently to share this powerful new secret with them. The resultant mistrust and concomitant arms race molded American-Soviet relations for the next forty-five years. Some writers have charged that the United States used the A-bombs on Japan partly to end the Pacific war before the Russians could come in and get a share in the peace settlement there, and also to intimidate Russia with a display of America's military might. Scholarly opinion weighs against this position. At the time the bombs were dropped, the Soviets remained potential allies in the Pacific. Atomic weapons were used to end the war quickly and unconditionally by any means available. At the same time, the A-bomb monopoly, and the U.S. refusal to give it up despite advice from its own scientists, fueled the Cold War and Russia's determination to have a nuclear capability.

In the United Nations, the Russians tried to get the United States to surrender its monopoly but failed. Between V-J Day and July 1946, the United States spent $13 billion on defense, partly for A-bomb tests and for super bombers (B-29s and B-36s) to deliver the weapon. The United States also acquired airfields around the world, threatening the Soviet Union. In response to Soviet pressure to end nuclear weapons entirely, on June 14, 1946, America proposed a plan (developed largely by Bernard Baruch) calling for an international body to control the world's uranium supply and license nuclear facilities. But the agency would be dominated by the United States, which would also keep its monopoly of nuclear weapons until some unspecified future date. To underline the point, the United States exploded test bombs at Bikini atoll seventeen days later. Despite warnings from scientists that the Soviets would have the bomb in three to five years, the American military believed their monopoly would last up to two decades. However, in 1949 the Russians successfully carried out a nuclear test, traumatizing the American public.

The Russians accused the United States and Britain of hypocrisy in suggesting their influence in the world was entirely benign. Although many peoples responded positively to U.S. leadership, the Americans, like the Soviets, also generated lasting hostility. This may surprise us when we think of America's postwar generosity. To encourage the building and preservation of free institutions, the United States shared its bounty with the world. Under the Marshall Plan alone (named after Secretary of State George C. Marshall, who proposed the idea in 1947), over $12 billion in aid was used to spark European economic recovery. By 1951, European industrial production had risen 64 percent. West Germany and Japan were rebuilt as models of free enterprise. Yet there was another side to the picture. Allied use of overwhelming force had ruined huge segments of the environment, including many of the world's cities, causing widespread resentment. Also, while war-ravaged countries that came under Anglo-American control were generally well administered, a lack of advance planning existed, as well as ineptitude and corruption, with thriving black markets involving soldiers and civilians approximating mafia operations in size and complexity. Graham Greene brought the scandal before a wide audience in his 1949 novel, *The Third Man*, exposing American involvement in the illicit drug trade within occupied Austria.

The Russians felt that the British and Americans, despite their rhetoric, blocked free choice in their spheres of influence. The trans-Atlantic allies distrusted European leftist groups and sometimes refused to work with them in forging the peace. During the conquest of North Africa in November 1942, the Allies cooperated with Admiral Jean-François Darlan, the Vichy governor and Nazi collaborator, snubbing the Free French forces under General Charles De Gaulle, seen as too leftist, thus earning De Gaulle's lasting enmity. Similarly, the United States never officially denounced Vichy or endorsed the radical antifascist Comité National de la Résistance.

In Italy, after Mussolini's overthrow, America and Britain excluded Russia from the settlement. Resistance members suspected of being communists were disarmed and sent home, allowing the pro-fascist administration of Marshal Pietro Badoglio to be installed. In Greece, the royalists, who had not resisted fascism, were similarly put in power, thwarting democratic hopes. Still, the degree of U.S. and British manipulations cannot be compared to Soviet repression: in the Western spheres, free elections and free-market economies were generally encouraged. Nevertheless, the demands of being a superpower forced Americans to subvert their own values. During the Cold War, the CIA funded clandestine operations to defeat left-wing movements in fifteen European countries, including Belgium, France, Germany, Italy, Portugal, Spain, Sweden, and Turkey.

The United States failed to understand the aspirations of progressive forces within developing nations emerging from colonialism, interpreting all left-wing movements as communist. This led to ill-conceived interventions in the internal affairs of sovereign nations to support right-wing, authoritarian groups hostile to communism, compromising America's wartime commitment to self-determination in Asia. During the war, American leaders repudiated European imperialism, pledging that they were not fighting to restore Western colonies.

Secretary of State Sumner Welles declared, "Our victory must bring in its train the liberation of all peoples. . . . The age of imperialism is ended" (Hess, 122–25).

This sentiment had momentous potential significance because Japanese victories early in the war had robbed Westerners of their aura of military invincibility, and independence movements sprouted across the region. Within two years of V-J Day, Britain withdrew from India, dooming French involvement in Indochina (Vietnam) and Dutch involvement in Indonesia. Ho Chi Minh, the Vietnamese nationalist leader, looked to the United States for help in resisting a French return, and he read the American Declaration of Independence at celebrations marking Japanese defeat in 1945. Yet, in 1950, the United States felt obliged to back the French after the 1949 shock of Russia exploding an atom bomb and North Korean communists invading South Korea in 1950.

The worst trauma to the American system came when China fell to communist forces under Mao Zedong in 1949. That this huge nation could succumb convinced Americans that communism was a disease so powerful it could penetrate the whole globe, and it intensified their commitment to the Cold War. Wartime propaganda had misled them into believing Chiang Kai-shek was a Western-style political leader bent on making China a democracy, whereas he was a feudal warlord with quasi-dictatorial powers. He led a government that was authoritarian, corrupt, and hated by many peasants. From 1953, the CIA funded raids by the remains of the nationalist army over the border from Burma, where it had taken refuge. This violation of Burmese sovereignty destabilized and divided that country, leading to civil war there.

Also in 1953, the CIA organized a coup to overthrow the legitimate Iranian government of Mohammad Mossadegh, installing the Shah as a repressive ruler, destructive meddling that haunts diplomatic relations to this day. A year later, the United States provoked a civil war in Guatemala, destroying the democratic government in favor of a reactionary dictator. In the Congo, 1960, Americans allegedly colluded in the assassination of President Patrice Lumumba, a progressive leader. In Cuba, after Fidel Castro came to power in 1959, overthrowing the tyrannical Batista regime, the United States attempted Castro's removal through assassination and the 1961 abortive Bay of Pigs invasion.

At one level, these illicit covert operations, often ruinous to the victim peoples, simply amounted to realpolitik, pragmatic exercises of power to guarantee U.S. political and economic dominance in key spheres of influence. Yet in another sense, American actions reflected a strong sense of moral superiority, justifying actions considered reprehensible when carried out by others. The seed of America's belief in its "exceptional" mission to save the world had been planted with the 1630 Massachusetts Bay colony that Puritan settlers saw as a beacon shining forth to guide the world. The nineteenth-century doctrine of Manifest Destiny vastly amplified this sense of a special purpose.

However, it was Americans' conception of their role in World War II that fully cemented into place a belief that the nation was so exceptional as a world leader it could legitimately undertake actions it condemned as immoral in others. In 1963, President John F. Kennedy, a war veteran who had sanctioned the Bay of Pigs invasion and other questionable covert operations, declared in soaring rhetoric, "We in this generation are—by destiny rather than choice—the watchmen on the walls of freedom." And when asked how American military intervention in Vietnam differed from earlier French involvement, Kennedy replied, "They were fighting for a colony, for an ignoble cause. We're fighting for freedom, to free them from the Communists" (Tuchman, 287). Kennedy failed to see that while America did not take ground to hold it as had previous Western colonial powers, its actions amounted to military and economic imperialism.

Until World War II, most covert operations were considered morally questionable, even reprehensible. Assassination, for example, was seen as a tool of anarchists and revolutionaries, not of legitimate states. Secretary Stimson for years objected to all covert intelligence work, reputedly saying, "Gentlemen don't read other people's mail" (Casey, 6). But the Axis appeared so evil that undercover operations became part of the game. Thus, Allied special operations assassinated the senior Nazi official Reinhard Heydrich, whose crimes included the ruthless extermination of "undesirables," a man credibly depicted as a werewolf by American poet Edna St. Vincent Millay. But once the concept of ends justifying the means became respectable, the genie could not be put back in the bottle.

America's moral myopia angered veteran Paul Fussell, who had seen action in the European theater. He stated the problem succinctly: "If for years you fancy that you are engaged in fighting utter evil, if every element and impulse of society is busy eradicating wickedness, before long you will come to believe that therefore you yourself must incarnate pure goodness." America's sense of virtue, said Fussell, obscured its own imperfections in "defending something pretty defective against something even more loathsome" (Fussell, 78). We need not go quite that far, but certainly the Western Allies in 1945 exhibited a degree of moral smugness.

They judged and condemned others, largely correctly, for cruel and wantonly brutal acts. But the Allies rarely pondered whether crimes committed by the enemy were universal in total war rather than the result of a unique perversity. The West did not analyze its own actions late in the war as the intensity of destruction escalated. For example, relatively few Americans questioned the morality of carpet bombing or dropping the atom bombs. General Douglas MacArthur, despite having opposed the nuclear attack, nevertheless announced in knightly diction during the Japanese war crimes trials that no escutcheon was more unsullied than that of the United States.

At Nuremberg, senior German officials were tried for war crimes, an important step in asserting the right of the international community to protect itself against aggression. But these men were tried primarily for crimes against other peoples; they were never made fully accountable before the bar of international justice for liquidating large elements of their own population. Moreover, both German and Japanese war criminals were protected from punishment if they had scientific knowledge valuable in working against the Soviets in, say, the nuclear rocket program. Thus, while the United States executed General Yamashita Tomoyuki in 1946 for war crimes he had not been aware of, it sheltered General Ishii Shiro, who had carried out medical experiments on live victims, since his work interested the U.S. Army. In 1983, the United States admitted it had employed Klaus Barbie, a notorious Nazi butcher, and later had helped him escape to Bolivia to avoid trial for war crimes committed in France.

That a sense of America's exceptional moral mission could coexist easily with a willingness to act from stark expediency is exemplified in General George Patton's thinking during his last months in Germany. Although he was sickened by the death camps, the general failed to understand the plight of the survivors, robbed of all possessions and cultural identity, worn down by malnutrition, disease, and ill treatment. He came to see the displaced as "a sub-human species without any of the cultural or social refinements of our time." His wartime hatred of the Nazis quickly dissipated, and he publicly advocated the employment of notorious Nazis in the struggle against communism in Europe. Patton was fired for making his views too public, but some of what he advocated became national policy (Farago, 515–20.)

The failure of World War II to bring a genuine peace had major consequences. The arms race ultimately ruined the Soviet system and severely damaged the U.S. economy. Each country acquired massive stockpiles of weapons, which were expensive to dispose of as they aged. In 1988, the United States possessed 37,657 nuclear weapons, the USSR had 17,656. Dangerous waste remained at abandoned arms plants, such as a decaying site in Fernald, Ohio, and at overseas bases in Europe and Asia, costing billions of dollars to clean up. The U.S. military estimated in 1992 that it had 309 polluted sites in Germany alone, with a bill for restoration possibly running to over $3 billion.

The Cold War undercut progressive sentiment in the United States. Even before the conflict ended, mainstream opinion shifted to the right. Partly this represented a reaction against the seemingly lax moral standards and social attitudes of wartime. However, the trend also reflected a determination by business, freed from the specter of depression, to curtail the social progressivism of the New Deal. The reactionary swing was symbolized by the dropping of liberal Vice President Henry Wallace as Roosevelt's running mate in the 1944 election in favor of the more moderate Harry S. Truman. FDR recognized America's growing conservatism and trimmed his policies accordingly.

Freedom of expression suffered in the postwar period. To have been a New Dealer, to have worked closely with the Russians during the war, or to currently oppose America's nuclear monopoly, might subject you to investigation by the House Un-American Activities Committee, established in 1938. Federal employees became subject to loyalty checks in 1947, leading to many firings on little evidence. Alleged communist infiltration became the scapegoat for some domestic problems, even juvenile delinquency among high schoolers.

Red scares went back to the nineteenth century, but the intense paranoia of the 1940s and 1950s owed much to the war. Propaganda depicted the Axis powers as a monolithic world conspiracy of slave states, without individual character or humanity. Ads talked of "an enemy who never sleeps," who was "right here in America," "always close, sneaking in the shadows." In 1943 John Roy Carlson published *Under Cover*, a book allegedly exposing over thirty-two nazi or fascist organizations in America. After the war, when communism replaced fascism as America's primary threat, the mantra of monolithic conspiracy easily adjusted to fit a new alien peril.

The end of the war brought disappointment for many American women. The trend of culling women from the job market, begun late in the war, continued into the peace. Between 1945 and early 1947, females lost 1 million factory jobs, 500,000 clerical jobs, and 400,000 sales positions. Females' share of paid work fell from 36 to 28 percent. Women often did not get unemployment relief, being labeled as leaving the workforce "voluntarily." Some job shrinkage occurred inevitably, as industry cut back to prevent a depression after the end of the war boom, but when the economy recovered and workers were recalled, women were largely left out. Detroit car makers now claimed that work women had done in the war was too heavy or technical for them. By April 1946, women's share of auto work was 7.5 percent, down from 25 percent during the war. The professions also reasserted male dominance: although 12 percent of 1945 entering medical students were women, only 5 percent of 1955 entering medical students were. Job cuts hurt lower-class families most because only by both spouses working could these families afford the luxuries America had become used to during the war.

Books on child welfare, looking back to the war, reinforced the push to send women home. They argued that absentee parents and group child care had damaged infants and produced juvenile delinquency. The cutting of federal day-care funds in March 1946 forced mothers to quit work. Dr. Benjamin Spock, perhaps the era's most influential pediatrician, argued initially that healthy children's development required full-time mothering. Women's magazines popularized his view, while movies showed the independent woman as socially dangerous. For example, in *Double Indemnity* (1944) and *The Postman Always Rings Twice* (1946), men who hooked up with the "new woman," bereft of traditional values, ended up ruined, even committing murder for these unnatural females. The marriage rate, a reflection of the urge to "settle down and have kids," jumped 50 percent in 1946 and remained 20 percent above the prewar rate for the rest of the decade.

The military also saw little role for women in its postwar establishment. After demobilization, female personnel fell from 266,000 to 14,000; in 1948, women were officially restricted to 2 percent of enlisted strength. Females found that promotion was difficult and that many specializations were barred to them. Unlike with men, female veterans' war service did not always help them in civilian life. Although nurses could easily get the same type of job they had in the military, employers rebuffed female mechanics, managers, and pilots. Some men actually thought that a woman with war service was, ipso facto, too independent or morally loose to be reliable. Certain federal agencies denied women veterans' benefits, and they were barred from the Veterans of Foreign Wars.

Homosexuals had benefited from wartime mobility, being able to meet others of like preference in the booming urban environment. Also, the military's attempt to identify gays through "scientific" testing shifted the discussion of homosexuality away from a crime against God to a discussion of it as a disease of biological origins, which represented an advance of sorts. Nevertheless, gays, like the independent women depicted in films, became a target of the postwar reaction to the freer atmosphere of wartime. Fear of and animosity towards gays increased when Alfred Kinsey, in 1948 and 1953, published two reports on American sexual behavior. He asserted that 50 percent of males and a somewhat lesser number of females felt erotic responses to their own sex. Although Kinsey argued his findings suggested persecution of gays should stop, critics went the other way: from about 1948 into the 1950s, homosexuals became a major subject of official investigations. They were denounced as perverts, child molesters, and communists. One Congressman claimed that the Kremlin had a list of American homosexuals it used to blackmail them into spying.

In 1950 homosexuals in federal service were targeted, and over sixty per month were dismissed. Homosexual veterans were frequently denied benefits under the GI Bill, such as college tuition, home loans, job training, and hospital care. Marty Klausner's homosexual discharge cost him his educational allowance. Then he could not get a job because his service record followed him around. "Why they don't round us all up and kill us I don't know," he said. However, some homosexual veterans finally got benefits with the help of the American Legion, the CIO, the NAACP, and the army surgeon general's office (Bérubé, 230–32).

* * *

Ethnic minorities found that fighting for democracy overseas did not necessarily parlay into civil liberties at home. Mississippi senator Theodore Bilbo said in 1947 that blacks should not be misled by wartime rhetoric into expecting equality or the end of segregation. African Americans and Hispanics faced discrimination in jobs, housing, and educational opportunities. Lowell Steward, a veteran black pilot, could not get work in civil aviation; at Long Beach Municipal Airport he was told "they didn't have no niggers at this base" (Terkel, 346–47). States like Alabama printed separate civics texts for minorities, omitting all reference to civil rights. In 1952, surveys showed that 87 percent of Southern black women and 65 percent of Southern black men had never voted. In 1948, fifteen states still had miscegenation laws, so that black veterans who had married white women overseas, or whites who had married Asians, could not return to these states. Only in 1967 did the Supreme Court strike down such laws.

Discrimination galled ethnic veterans who found their services ignored and their rights withheld. Only 7.5 percent of veterans in the South who received job training through the GI Bill were black, even though they represented 33 percent of Southern servicemen. Blacks who reacted against such discrimination were labeled communist agitators, and the Ku Klux Klan was revived to oppose these "militants." On July 20, 1946, Macio Snipes, a veteran and the only black to vote in his Georgia district primary, was gunned down in one of several racial murders.

The flagrant withholding of domestic freedoms from those who had fought for them overseas produced a growing minority demand for civil rights. Membership in the National Association for the Advancement of Colored People (NAACP) grew from 50,556 in 1940 to 450,000 by 1946. James Baldwin, the distinguished African American writer, believed that the postwar betrayal of the hope for equality brought on the violent clashes of the 1960s. Picture, he said, a soldier coming home: stand in his shoes as he searches for a job, or a place to live; sit in his seat on segregated buses; see, through his eyes, the signs reading 'White' and 'Colored.' Such experiences, warned Baldwin, would produce "the fire next time," America burning. White Americans, he charged, acted as if unaware both of the exemplary war service of blacks and the injustices perpetrated on them when they returned. In a provocative comment, Baldwin postulated that this pretended innocence in itself constituted a racial crime.

We may ask how racism of any kind could have continued when, seemingly, we had just fought the most costly war in history to destroy authoritarian systems making claims to ethnic superiority? But we must understand that, as Paul Fussell said, our moral superiority to these regimes was relative only. We have seen that, before the war, blacks, Hispanics, and Jews were broadly discriminated against. Let us take anti-Semitism as a case study. In much of America, as in Europe, anti-Semitism was virulent during the 1930s and 1940s. Jews were excluded from the best clubs and hotels. Employers could practice subtle discrimination because it was legal to ask an applicant's religion. Right-wing commentators who embraced many tenets of nazism attacked Jews in the media. The influential media personality Father Charles E. Coughlin accused Jewish families like the Rothschilds of using their wealth to dominate the media, business, and banking in a conspiracy to control America. His views were echoed on the street by people like Sheril Cunning's grandfather who, when he saw a big Jewish party in a restaurant, would say, "The kikes are taking over" (Terkel 233).

Nazi racism per se did not provoke World War II: rather, the catalyst was Hitler's aggression against other sovereign states, beginning with Poland. No state went to war to prevent the maltreatment of "undesirables" within the German population. And saving concentration camp victims was not a primary aim of the Allies, who showed a degree of callousness toward Hitler's victims. Neither Britain nor America did much during the Nazi era to help Jews fleeing persecution. The U.S. Immigration Act of 1924 restricted the number of applicants who could enter the country annually. Despite pleas from Jewish and humanitarian groups, the quota was not liberalized to help fugitives. As a result, only 120,000 Jews entered the United States from 1933 to 1941; many thousands more were turned away. Only in January 1944 were some thousands beyond the quota admitted. This insensitivity affected other wartime policies. At the 1943 Moscow Conference, Hitler's treatment of Jews went unmentioned, although his other crimes were listed.

In defeated Germany, some American military personnel came to feel closer to the Germans than to the camp inmates. As early as September 1945, an army survey showed that 22 percent of GIs thought the Nazi treatment of Jews justified; another 10 percent were unsure. In March 1946, *Reader's Digest* declared that the reason "so many GIs like the Germans best" was that they were cleaner and friendlier than most Europeans. GIs brought their prejudices back with them. At home, Jews were accused of avoiding the draft, and gentiles harassed Jewish soldiers. Many of Arno Mayer's fellow officers were anti-Semitic; once he was handed a paper with the lines, "When we finish with the Germans and the Japs / We'll come back and kill the Jews and the blacks" (Terkel, 470).

The myth of national unity in World War II blinded many Americans to the continuing divisions within their society. Some, bewildered by the civic unrest that came to a head in the 1960s, blamed the turmoil on the youth of that era, suggesting that an apparently happy and united society suddenly and mysteriously came unglued. In fact, the bill for ethnic prejudice that had been building since the war and beyond simply came due.

Another myth of the 1940s versus the 1960s and 1970s was that while combat veterans from Vietnam and later wars suffered long-term adjustment problems,

World War II vets came home to enjoy prosperity quietly, satisfied about their service, with few qualms about the war. This scenario oversimplified the reality. Many veterans of the big war, particularly the majority who never saw combat, adjusted quickly. But some suffered an anguish that damaged their lives and those of their families. For some, the stress never went away.

Veterans with physical wounds sometimes took years to recover or die. Stan Baker, a GI from Washington State, had severe leg wounds from a machine gun burst that failed to heal. They kept forming blood clots. Seven years after the war, a clot broke away and moved to the heart, killing him. Some had disfigurements to cope with. A nurse recalled one hospitalized pilot during 1945 who was so badly burned that he was unrecognizable. Beside his bed he kept a photo of himself before his injuries, swearing he would never get up until he looked like that again. Civilians tried to sympathize but sometimes could not stomach it. The wife of a man who had lost one side of his face, planned to divorce him. There was hypocrisy regarding America's returning heroes. One woman recalled that, when a cousin became engaged to a GI with a missing leg, the family made a fuss over him at dinner but later asked, "Wouldn't you think she'd know better than to marry a cripple?" (Terkel, 235).

Many combat veterans endured mental wounds. Often, survivors could function but had to overcome nervous reactions to specific traumatic stimuli. Men who had faced land mines could not walk on grass for years afterward. One pilot had to pull off the road when his car tires thwacked on concrete joints, resembling flak bursts. Another vet dived under his in-laws' dining table when a plane buzzed low overhead. George Wheeler of the 8th Armored Division could not stand jackhammering, reminiscent of a 50-caliber machine gun. Some overcame these difficulties comparatively quickly. Others continued to suffer. Ferdinand Huber of the 99th Infantry Division said it was more than a decade before he could discuss the war without shaking. Even in 1967, a paratrooper who had nearly drowned on a drop in Normandy frequently leapt out of bed, sweating from nightmares. In the 1980s, marine veteran William Manchester still chose seats in restaurants giving maximum protection from hostile fire.

John Garcia, who killed a woman and child he mistook for enemy troops, said in 1985: "That hounds me. I still feel I committed murder" (Terkel, 21). Captain Charles Butler McVay III, commander of the USS Indianapolis, sunk by a Japanese submarine on July 30, 1945, shot himself on November 6, 1968. Although cleared of all wrongdoing, McVay was haunted by the disaster, especially as he still received hate mail accusing him of murder. "*I can't take this*" said his suicide note (Stanton, 274). In 1990, 25 percent of patients still in veterans' hospitals from the war had psychological wounds. What they had witnessed had driven them into permanent retreat or dissociation from the world. As late as 2005, Ed Wood, badly hurt by a shell burst in Normandy in September 1944, still suffered from post-traumatic stress disorder (PTSD): "my life has been crippled by the emotional and physical consequences of that wound," he believed (Wood, 55). At 85, in 2009, Joseph E. Garland of the 45th Infantry Division, who had suffered survivor guilt since the war, said, "I confess in the recollection of it all to a tinge of what we now call post-traumatic stress disorder" (Garland, xiii–xv).

Recently, medicine has made rapid advances in understanding the connection between abnormal behavior and a particular physical wound: PTSD is linked to traumatic brain injury (TBI), physiological damage causing unstable, aggressive behavior. The Walter Reed National Military Medical Center now studies these conditions in tandem. TBI is usually caused by brain concussions. Physicians focus on this problem because, in recent wars, concussions from insurgents' improvised explosive devices (IEDs) have become ubiquitous on the battlefield. The Defense and Veterans Brain Injury Center estimated in 2014 that U.S. soldiers have suffered over 265,000 TBIs in the last twelve years. (The National Football League is also increasingly concerned about advanced brain damage in players, seemingly traceable to multiple concussions.) Simply put, the condition occurs because the brain is not fixed rigidly in place; it has elasticity and moves within the skull, a little like a Jell-O mold. When the brain is slammed into the hard skull bone, damage ensues, leading to nerve degeneration. The injury may or may not heal over time.

This leads us to reconsider the ramifications of the large number of concussions sustained by combatants during World War II. Audie Murphy, America's most decorated soldier, provides an arresting case. From poor circumstances in Texas, the slightly built, soft-spoken Murphy fought in north Africa, Sicily, Italy, southern France, and Germany, rising from private to lieutenant. He earned thirty-three military awards, including the Congressional Medal of Honor. In peacetime, he became a seemingly successful film actor, appearing in some forty-three movies. Freckled, boyishly handsome, Murphy appeared to be the complete rags to riches success story, appearing on covers of magazines with his first wife, Wanda, as the perfect American couple. However, behind the scenes, all was far from well. Murphy endured chronic combat fatigue during the latter stages of fighting and may have lost the urge for self-preservation, recklessly exposing himself to perform some of the deeds that made him a hero.

He also suffered multiple concussions. In the 1943 Sicily campaign, for example, a high impact 20-mm round knocked him unconscious, provoking nose bleeds that lasted a decade. In another incident that year, a mortar shell landed nearby, causing serious injury, killing two men and wounding three others. Twice in January 1945 he sustained concussions, from a mortar round that also lacerated his legs and from a shell blast that knocked him flat. Conventional medical wisdom held that the effects of these blows to the brain would go away with time. Murphy's postwar behavior suggests otherwise.

He suffered from prolonged physical lassitude punctuated by bouts of erratic violence. Smiling good humor instantly switched to irascibility. When angered, he threatened his wife, friends, film directors, and crew, even passing strangers, with a Colt 45, his habitual companion. He loved guns. His volatility led to frequent fistfights over trivial slights. He once shot holes in Wanda's apartment door to prove she could not hide from him. She felt that "if I didn't wind up in the nut house, I'd wind up in the grave" (Graham, 189). At other times, he would stick a gun in his own mouth, swearing he could no longer live with the misery of struggling to act normally in boring, conventional, postwar America. The erstwhile hero suffered from nightmares, insomnia, drug addiction, and an inability to look after money. A fatal plane crash in 1971 ended his self-destructive spiral into financial and personal ruin. Murphy believed himself a late war casualty, a refugee from the law of averages facing the combat soldier.

Given this reality of abnormal, anguish-laden behavior, why is it popularly believed that World War II combat veterans, unlike participants in later wars, escaped lasting injury from mental wounds? Partly, this is simply a failure to understand the statistical profile of the fighting forces. In World War II, only 5 percent of personnel saw combat; the overwhelming percentage never entered harm's way. By Vietnam, the figure for combat exposure had jumped to 50 percent. Since 2001, 70 percent of soldiers fighting the War on Terror have experienced some form of combat. There is no safe rear area anymore in territory saturated by insurgents; most personnel endure a 24-7, 360-degree exposure to danger: at any time, they may be wounded or killed by sniper fire or IEDs that detonate unexpectedly, a vulnerability that grinds on the nervous system. Consequently, the number suffering emotional damage has expanded.

Further, we have been slow to document abnormal behavior among World War II vets because families hushed up problems in an era when alcoholism and family abuse were swept under the rug. Many civilians had no wish to understand or tolerate mental wounds, putting them down to innate character deficiencies. Steve Maharidge, a marine veteran who suffered PTSD into the twenty-first century, remained subject to violent rages, abusing his family and getting into fights. He also had an unstable job record, stealing merchandise to cover his gambling debts. A female neighbor in Cleveland, Ohio, whose son perished, screamed at Maharidge, "Why'd you come back and not _____! The good ones died over there" (Maharidge, xii, 11).

Conventional thinking in the 1940s and 50s held that only weak men talked about mental distress. Charles Taylor warned his wife before demobilization he would not discuss the war, just try to be a regular guy. Most vets, he said, would rather leave the war years blank. An American, giving guided tours of the Normandy battlefields to veterans returning to the scenes in old age, told author Doris Lessing that most had never told their wives what they went through.

Other survivors wanted to talk but feared they would be seen as monsters by civilians unfamiliar with the dynamics of real war. To protect his old buddies, one sergeant gave rookie replacements the most dangerous assignments, such as walking point. Unused to pinpointing approaching danger, they got killed quickly. Afterward, the noncom felt badly, wanting to confide in his wife about the predicament, but he was afraid he would seem monstrous. A GI who guarded German POWs late in the war admitted they were deliberately starved in revenge for Nazi crimes: "We sometimes slipped over the boundary of civilized behavior and resembled to some extent what we were fighting against" (Field, Letter to the Editor). Another said that he witnessed atrocities the public tried to gloss over. When passions cooled, such actions haunted participants.

Psychologists reinforced the veterans' reticence, seeing guilt feelings as retrogressive, a hindrance to a life-affirming philosophy. "Even the simplest soldier," said veteran J. Glenn Gray, "suspects that it is unpopular today to be burdened with guilt" (Gray, 174 and 23–24). Between October 1945 and June 1946, nearly 3 million personnel were demobilized. Given the pace, people needed to believe readjustment would be smooth and seamless. The easiest thing was to assume "our boys" had not changed. A veteran recalled Red Cross workers distributing candy and comics to returning troops as though they were still the adolescents that had gone to war. Magazines promoted the idea of a quick fix, *Good Housekeeping* telling wives that their husbands should stop "oppressive remembering" in two to three weeks. Even the army, in its 1946 educational documentary *Let There Be Light*, predicted most men should be doing well in eight to ten weeks.

Such predictions were disingenuous. As veteran James Jones put it, men who had "once seen something animal within themselves that terrified them" would take years to get over the shock (Jones, 339). Some veterans fled human society, living in the backwoods. Others made family life miserable. In trying to keep their trauma bottled up inside, they drank, gambled, suffered paralyzing depression, and became violent. One paratrooper's wife just sat holding him for hours while he struggled with the shakes. Afterward, he started beating her and the children. He "became a brute," and she divorced him (Terkel, 108). In 1992, another woman said of her brother, a Pacific veteran, that the family never understood him after he came home. He left as a bright, energetic eighteen-year-old, returning a lifeless alcoholic. He got married but quickly divorced, dying of cirrhosis of the liver at thirty-four.

*   *   *

Inevitably, marriages suffered great stress. Soldiers overseas had often subsisted mentally on an idealized image of home, frozen in time. John M. Wright notified his wife to expect a Rip Van Winkle on his return. But the land and its people had changed irrevocably. Wives were older and less perfect than the dream image. Veterans were sharply disappointed. Struggling through enormous adjustments, spouses coped with husbands who seemed hostile strangers. Although during the war, many women had discovered hidden abilities in themselves, heightening their self-confidence, psychologists warned them to downplay these competencies, assuaging the bruised male ego. *House Beautiful* told the wife to remember that her spouse headed the household again. Her task entailed making sure the home ran to his specifications. This proved a tall order, given the paradoxical nature of woman's role: she was to be meek and attentive, but if the man failed to get back to work and normal functioning, she was to push him forward.

Women were warned that returning soldiers and their children might have trouble relating to each other, being essentially strangers. Given the more relaxed moral standards of wartime, some men wondered if they actually had fathered their kids. Some fathers, whose only adult experience was of the services, had no parental approach to fall back on other than military discipline, treating boys especially as little soldiers in training, telling them to stand up straight or get haircuts. Breaking rules of behavior could incur severe punishments. When young Tom Mathews would not jump off a tall roof to please his paratrooper father, the ex-lieutenant stalked away, shouting, "No son of mine is a coward." Tom's mother also endured verbal abuse, her husband screaming, "Goddammit. You've spoiled my son." The boy "thought, on balance, that my life would be off to a better start if only the Germans had killed him" (Mathews, 4 and 10). Some relationships healed over time, but other men remained permanently estranged from their children's emotional lives.

A further strain on veterans and their dependents was that immediately after the war they were three times as likely as civilians to be unemployed. Massachusetts reported 67,000 unemployed former servicemen by March 1946. This meant that many couples, separated during the war, now had to share life with in-laws under trying conditions. In January 1946, 60 percent of married veterans in the Northeast lacked their own homes. Over a million Americans married while overseas, and some relationships faced special problems. The foreign bride of a GI could have trouble adjusting to American life and might face hostility if German or Japanese. Some wives, expecting the America of Hollywood films, were shocked by the reality, especially of rural life. One French girl expected *Gone with the Wind* but got a Georgia sharecropper's cabin without toilet or running water. Interracial couples, often denied immigration papers, had to live abroad. The daunting issues facing military marriages led to an unusually high failure rate. By late 1945, divorces for veterans under forty-five years old reached one in twenty-nine, compared to one in sixty for civilians.

Widows and mothers of dead or mutilated service personnel faced particular stresses. Many widows found that they were no longer welcome at social gatherings, an embarrassing reminder that the war years had not been good for everyone. Although widows' pensions were inadequate at $50 a month (rising to a maximum of $100 if one had several children, versus $150 a month for a disabled vet), businesses balked at hiring single mothers, maintaining they should be at home caring for family full time. Those who could find jobs often led very hard lives. Veronica Coleman, whose husband Bob was killed in 1944, said in a 1978 interview: "I've worked all my life, supported my daughter, made up for what the Army didn't give, which wasn't too much. To keep close to her I went to factory work where I could name my own hours, go to work after she went to school and be home when she came back." She lamented "the life that never was" for her and Bob, blotted out by a German shell thirty-four years earlier (Garland, 442).

Because the forces preferred to induct single men, mothers and fathers were four times more likely to be bereaved than were soldiers' wives. This also meant that mothers, even more than spouses, became full-time nurses of the disabled. The Pentagon bluntly stated it had neither the psychiatric personnel nor the facilities to give most mental patients the time and care needed. Fenton Grahnert, a Pacific veteran, recalled that "they turned us—eight and a half, nine million people loose from the military after World War II. Just kicked your ass out in the street with not a goddam penny of psychiatric help or nothing" (Maharidge, 113). Most women, untrained to deal with psychological injuries, lived under severe strain, imposed by coping with erratic behavior of loved ones.

During the war, over 125,000 Americans were taken prisoner. Some were never repatriated, fate unknown. Also, in 1946, the Pentagon listed about 44,000 personnel still officially missing in action. Probably most were dead, obliterated by exploding rounds, flame throwers, plane crashes, drownings. But for the families of absent loved ones, lack of closure prolonged the grieving process. Wives of missing men occupied a particularly painful position, unable to get on with trying to build a new life in case husbands might return, living in a state of indefinite suspension that ended years later in recognition that the ghost at the table was not returning.

Society offered veterans a helping hand through the GI Bill, enacted in 1944. This legislation aided many veterans, giving them middle-class status they might not have achieved otherwise. Officially labeled the Serviceman's Readjustment Act, the bill guaranteed veterans fifty-two weeks of unemployment benefits, cheap housing and other loans, medical assistance, and up to four years of education or job training. Under the bill, over 8 million veterans got education or training, easing the pressure on the job market and ultimately helping their career potential. Veterans, used to disciplined work habits, achieved higher educational levels than their civilian peers. By 1946, 1.5 million were in college. Looking back, the vice president of a Chicago publishing firm believed "the GI Bill made all the difference in the world" for him, as he "could never have afforded college" (Terkel, 55, also 135–37).

Most Americans agreed that the bill was warranted and did great good, but some worried that this extensive entitlement program for one segment of society could prove the thin wedge of socialism. Historian Dixon Wecter warned of this in a 1944 essay. In the same year, Robert J. Watt, head of the American Federation of Labor, predicted that veterans' preferred status encouraged minorities to claim special entitlements. Such views are debatable. But it is true that veterans' benefits became the single most expensive social welfare legislation in the national budget, increasing the original cost of the war by over 125 percent. By 1950, veterans' benefits represented 30 percent of public social welfare spending, and costs continued to grow. In 1990, more than half the men over age sixty-five were veterans, amounting to 7.2 million recipients of special medical and pension benefits.

The GI Bill affected education, helping to make higher education a normal part of the American dream. On the positive side, it allowed far more people to go to college. But some argued it lowered college standards and curriculum content. Veterans often wanted strictly vocational courses, continuing movement away from the liberal arts. Colleges speeded up programs for veterans, already impeded by the war. George H. W. Bush finished Yale in under three years. Professors sometimes avoided flunking veterans, and administrators needed their federal funds, increasing grade inflation. Universities became increasingly dependent on the GI Bill and other military-related grants, diminishing their academic independence and drawing them into the growing military-industrial-government complex. In the early 1950s, 99.5 percent of federal aid to higher education was military related.

At its best, the GI Bill helped immensely to create a new, aspiring middle class, achieving educational and income goals inconceivable a generation before. At the same time, critics said, the bill added to the middle class an element that had arrived too quickly for real sophistication, proving dull, anti-intellectual, obsessed with buying correctly and appearing respectable. It lived in mass suburbs with repetitious architecture (little boxes made of ticky-tacky) and an artificial culture based on aggressive Americanism and distrust of eccentrics and outsiders. It was insecure in its newfound comfort, uptight, and hostile to nonconformists. Obsession with the flag as a precious symbol of Americanism, playing the national anthem at ball games, and other overt manifestations of patriotism that dated from the war period became settled traditions of white middle-class life.

Whatever the role of the GI Bill, certainly the war encouraged what William H. Whyte, an editor of *Fortune* magazine, called organization culture: a trend toward bureaucracy, standardization, regulation, and conformity in everything from clothing to personal values to political candidates. Uniformity began to increase when millions of Americans came of age in the country's largest organization, the armed forces: used to military discipline, they tended to be passive workers, waiting for orders. To a degree inconceivable a generation earlier, government regulation of public activities by regulatory agencies expanded enormously, intruding into citizens' lives through such offices as the Internal Revenue Service. Big business, too, imposed standardization and conformity through its products and personnel procedures.

After a victorious war, the military became a success model, and corporations adopted military-style hierarchical management. James Jones, a veteran, writer, and social critic, maintained that the war produced a demand for "team players" with a related loss of respect for individualism (Jones, 474). The sociologist David Riesman thought that by 1950 pressure to conform to mass opinion produced management, not leadership, aiming to preserve the status quo and discourage unpopular decisions or new directions unsanctioned by opinion polls. He noted that during the war even generals ceased being leaders, avoiding unpleasant truths and controversial positions, deferring to the popular media. In this atmosphere, America would produce "other-directed" youth, thinking and acting not according to the dictates of inner voices but bowing to peer pressure. Riesman called Americans "the lonely crowd" (Riesman, 130–31, 21).

The most famous exposition of conformity to authority as a primary value was Herman Wouk's *The Caine Mutiny* (1951), a fictional story of an American minesweeper whose captain, Queeg, ended exhausted and mentally wrecked due to prolonged war service. During a storm threatening to capsize the boat, he froze and had to be relieved of command by his first officer, Maryk. The lieutenant was tried for mutiny and acquitted, but Wouk made it clear that Maryk wrongly challenged the captain. Organizational ethics demanded obedience even to incompetents representing authority.

Whyte criticized Wouk, fearing such views robbed America of needed personal initiative, self-reliance, and willingness to take business risks: "Here, certainly, is an outstanding denial of individual responsibility. The system is presented as having such a mystique that apparent evil becomes a kind of good." Whyte also noted that Wouk's real villain was not the mad captain but the intellectual officer, Keefer, who first pointed out the captain's insanity, encouraging other officers to question the command structure. Keefer was "too clever to be wise." Wouk's message was: better to be an average team player who fits into the organization than an intellectual critic or a whistle-blower (Whyte, 245–46). Implicitly, *The Caine Mutiny* endorsed early Cold War suppression of dissent and questioning of the system.

Ironically, the war that brought prosperity and a burgeoning middle class also nurtured conformity and intolerant Americanism. More people became educated, but materialism increased, as did contempt for the humanities. But these and other more negative outcomes would be smothered in the rhetoric of a legend suggesting Americans who fought the war and molded the peace nurtured a golden age, the best era ever in human history. We must now turn to the mythologizing of the war and why simplifications of a complex reality appealed to the public for so long.

CHAPTER SEVEN

The Life Cycle of a Myth

In 1998, the prominent television journalist Tom Brokaw, in a breathtakingly panoramic judgment, declared America's World War II generation to be "the greatest generation any society has produced" (Brokaw, xxx). The year also saw President Bill Clinton's liaison with White House intern Monica Lewinsky and the release of Steven Spielberg's movie *Saving Private Ryan*, a fictional drama set in 1944 Normandy. These events, coming together, in different ways fed into a powerful myth about World War II as America's Good War, a myth that reached its crowning height in the last years of the twentieth and the first years of the twenty-first centuries.

Brokaw was not ignorant of American history. He knew World War II was a complex event in which much we did was good and admirable. But mistakes were made, and there were blemishes. At times, such as in the air war and Pacific ground fighting, we matched our opponents in ferocity. We inaugurated nuclear weapons. Domestically, ethnic and gender discrimination marred society. Brokaw consciously simplified this complex reality to promote a myth. He drew inspiration from Stephen E. Ambrose, a major professional historian who became increasingly selective in his work on World War II, extolling American virtues at the expense of framing a complete picture. Both authors built upon a legend of World War II as the Good War that had been growing for the previous half century in books, movies, and political and editorial statements. Its roots were in the war itself, so we start at that beginning. Later, I examine how myth can mislead in ways that have real-world consequences. And I consider why the story of the best war ever may now be in eclipse.

Myths are ways we try to shape a usable past to help in directing present actions and setting our future course. They are constructive unless, in narrowing our focus, we stray too far from the complex patterns of history and begin weaving fantasy. In World War II, only positive aspects of the war received mainstream attention, setting a pattern for interpreting the war's meaning. The process was simple. All belligerent nations filtered the information their peoples received, suppressing reports of blunders or atrocities by their own side. Journalists voluntarily self-censored to assist the war effort. Canadian reporter Charles Lynch spoke for the international press corps when he admitted, "We were cheerleaders." Perhaps this was necessary, he felt, but "it wasn't good journalism. It wasn't journalism at all" (Knightley, 332–33).

Civilians blocked out the war's harsher aspects. Citizens angrily denounced the military for releasing pictures of American corpses at Tarawa. When a plastic surgery hospital in Pasadena, California, allowed disfigured patients to go downtown, residents demanded they be kept out of sight. While some parts of reality were erased, others were enlarged to flatter the military edifice. For example, in one two-year period, General Douglas MacArthur reported 200,000 enemy killed for only 122 Allied lost. After he was driven from the Philippines, MacArthur's press staff manufactured his seemingly spontaneous line, "I shall return." When he did come back, the dramatic scene of him wading ashore was shot repeatedly, on different beaches, to achieve the best effect. Fifty cameramen were on hand when General Dwight Eisenhower and his staff went ashore in Normandy, and they were told which profiles to shoot. General George Patton's rousing speeches to the troops were carefully staged, as were some of his jeep rides to the front. General Mark Clark, a notorious publicity hound, risked soldiers' lives by rushing mop-up operations in Rome to have a photo-op at the coliseum.

The media-created, larger-than-life image of the brass was exploited in postwar movies, such as *The Longest Day* (1962), a triumphalist cinemascope epic about D-Day in which prominent film stars played the leading generals. In *Patton* (1970), George C. Scott and Patton melded into one screen persona, as both were movie stars. However, the most enduring heroic war movies focused on ordinary soldiers, the platoon. This genre began in the war to promote national solidity and suggest the vitality of a diverse democracy pitted against enemies boasting of racial purity. Platoon movies portrayed American units as melting pots (excluding minorities), where, say, a Midwestern office worker, a Southern farm boy, a New York Italian, and a Boston intellectual found common strength, led by a tough professional sergeant. Robert Taylor set the tone in *Bataan* (1943).

The iconic platoon movie was *Sands of Iwo Jima* (1949), starring John Wayne as the hard-bitten Sergeant Stryker leading a band of neophytes from boyhood to manhood. The movie had a gritty strength, and Stryker was no plaster saint, a divorcee estranged from his family. But he was also a towering figure in the heroic mold.

Books produced in the war mainly avoided questioning Allied virtue and presented a sanitized version of combat. Thomas R. St. George's *C/O Postmaster* (1943) was an inane adventure story, ending prior to heavy fighting. His GIs' realization that some will die only makes them tougher. In *An American Guerrilla in the Philippines* (1945), journalist Ira Wolfert penned a laudatory biography of David Richardson, who organized guerrilla attacks on the Japanese. Tellingly, Wolfert extolled Richardson's simplicity: "Like most Americans, Richardson's politics are the politics of a child. He wants things in his life to be as nice as they can be. When they aren't he wants to know the reasons, and if he doesn't like the reasons he'll fight" (Wolfert, v–vi).

Some postwar writers who had seen the massive destruction tried for literary authenticity. John Hersey, in *Hiroshima* (1946), exposed the lasting effects of radiation. He touched many people but others still thought the Japanese got what they deserved; the book just made them more fearful about a possible Russian nuclear program. Vets like James Jones in *The Thin Red Line* (1962) and Norman Mailer in *The Naked and the Dead* (1948) described combat's horror, including fragging (murder) of one's own side. Mailer projected America as growing militarist due to the conflict. The authors' realistic use of obscene army language offended many, and others called them sick for their gritty, seemingly unpatriotic depictions.

Most people got their war stories from movies that diluted reality. James A. Michener's biting memoir, *Tales of the South Pacific* (1947), was filmed as a musical, *South Pacific*, in 1958. The stage version retained some criticism of military sexism, but the steamy jungle, full of pests and diseases, oppressively foreboding, became a tropical paradise. Glamorous nurses wore short shorts and made girly talk. An officer about to marry a native girl was conveniently killed (offstage) so that the audience need not think about the consequences of this mixed marriage. Veteran Irwin Shaw's novel *The Young Lions* (1948) found no redemption in the plight of youngsters sent to kill. But the 1958 film version softened the scenes of battle and strove for transcendence through Allied victory.

There were more biting movies: *The Victors* (1963) offered a critique of the powerful men who waged war. *The Big Red One* (1980), made by veteran Samuel Fuller, suggested the only triumph in war was survival, although it also extended the platoon motif, with Lee Marvin playing the tough noncom turning boys into men. Veterans Joseph Heller, in *Catch-22* (1961; filmed 1970), and

Kurt Vonnegut Jr., in *Slaughterhouse-Five* (1969; filmed 1972), took aim at romanticization of the war. Heller depicted the strain on bomber crews led by callous generals obsessed with promotion. Vonnegut portrayed badly led, hapless, bewildered green soldiers taken prisoner in the Bulge and bombed by their own side in Dresden. However, their dark humor seemed more appropriate to the Vietnam era, and they were not taken seriously as World War II writers. The tide ran against frank film criticism. The release of *Come See the Paradise* (1990), a moving drama detailing the harsh treatment of Japanese Americans in the war, was delayed when the Gulf War began.

As generations grew up unfamiliar with the 1940s, film became less accurate. The 1990 drama *Memphis Belle* remade the stark 1943 documentary *The Memphis Belle*, which had been shot on the bomber's last mission over Germany. The later movie is an action fantasy, using special effects to suggest the plane survives inconceivable levels of damage, while the crew indulge in preposterous heroics. Yet the reviews were good. The *Cincinnati Enquirer* (October 14, 1990) said it was packed with "true heroism and good old-fashioned patriotism." The star, Matthew Modine, was quoted as saying the heroics showed "a kind of value that doesn't exist today. Today there's a lot of shirking of responsibility."

Modine's comment reflects an increasing trend to couple praise of the war generation with criticism of later Americans. Why? World War II was an outright victory. Later conflicts had conditional endings: Korea was a stalemate, Vietnam a defeat. America's power seemed eroded. The United States shifted from the world's leading creditor to a debtor nation. Few allies supported the Americans in Vietnam, and many turned away from military action as a solution to world problems. At home, antiwar protests and civil rights marches rocked suburban America's equanimity. Living in a world more complex and difficult to handle, it became easy to project the 1940s as a golden age when everything seemed straightforward and worked out better. At a time when many ordinary Americans felt demoralized, Ronald Reagan, a figure from the Good War, took the presidency and brought back pride when the Berlin Wall fell and the Soviet Union crumbled.

Reagan asserted American greatness as a faith conquering doubt: we were without warts and blemishes, so whatever we did was right. Although, together with John Wayne, he had not fought in World War II, he came to believe he had, and many Americans believed with him. The renowned African American writer James Baldwin had Reagan in mind when he told the National Press Club in Washington, DC, that distorting history was now acceptable so long as your message was sincere and avoided disturbing questioning. By the late 1980s and 90s, veneration of the war generation, based on simplification of the 1940s, had reached the proportions of ancestor worship.

Many hoped the Gulf War of 1990, precipitated by Iraqi occupation of Kuwait, would allow us, as a side benefit, to relive our era of greatest triumph. George H. W. Bush, president and commander-in-chief, carried a World War II history with him on *Air Force One* during the crisis. The media called Saddam Hussein a new Hitler, and *TV Guide* compared theater commander Norman Schwarzkopf to Winston Churchill. CBS called him John Wayne taking on the Iraqis. However, having carried out the United Nations mandate to drive the Iraqis from Kuwait, the president took the humane and statesmanlike decision to end the war short of taking Baghdad. The one-sided slaughter became so bloody that pilots balked at flying missions they called turkey shoots. Bush, a Pacific theater veteran, knew all about slaughter. And by not toppling Hussein, he retained the delicate balance of power in the region between Iraq and Iran. A satisfied president said we had finally kicked the Vietnam syndrome, meaning America was back on its winning streak. But this limited victory by no means satisfied everyone; they wanted an outright triumph, echoing 1945. This frustration would fester.

Those disappointed that the Gulf War had fallen short of realizing the dream of reliving the best war ever were left asking questions. Paul Taylor of the *Washington Post* wondered morosely if America's national genius was dying along with the Greatest Generation. The election of Bill Clinton as president in 1992, welcomed by many, exacerbated the gloom of some. Jonathan Alter, in a May 1994 *Newsweek*, predicted the World War II generation's achievements would far surpass any of Clinton's generation. This self-immolation (Alter was of the younger generation) became typical of a growing trend among sons of World War II fathers. As they reached middle age and their fathers grew old (by 2005 one thousand vets died per day), men who had rebelled in the 1960s against their seemingly conformist fathers, challenging the Vietnam war and unthinking allegiance, came to regret their stance. Their mea culpa struck a responsive chord when Stephen Ambrose turned to venerating ordinary World War II soldiers as a band of buddies, admirable common men who quietly got the job done.

Let us go, then, to Ambrose's pivotal work. Born in 1936 and dying in 2002, Ambrose was a leading historian of his generation. His early work, particularly on the Civil War, had been outstandingly researched and balanced in judgment. During his career, however, his approach underwent a sea change. He began as a liberal student, studying under professors he later dubbed academic snobs, looking down on ordinary people in mid-twentieth-century America as conformist organization men. His teachers assigned texts from William H. Whyte and David Riesman, and they criticized President Eisenhower as an uninspired product of military bureaucracy. As a young man, Ambrose energetically opposed the

Vietnam War. There might be an implicit criticism here of his father, a physician in the Pacific theater.

However, in 1989, Ambrose became head of the Eisenhower Center at the University of New Orleans. He wrote extensively on Ike, including the authorized biography. This new intellectual exposure, along with age, made him more conservative. In that seminal year, 1998, he said World War II produced unique fighting spirit and team work, adding, "In these days of the 'me generation' and instant gratification, it is no wonder that those of us over fifty-five years of age look back with a certain nostalgia and think of it as 'the good war'" (Ambrose, *Americans*, 189). This kind of gratuitous simplification colored some of his later thinking. Between 1992 and 1998 Ambrose produced a series of books focusing mainly on American forces in Europe, particularly in Normandy. Much of this work was characterized by valuable insights and fine writing. But he also focused narrowly and repeatedly on two points.

First, he overstated the importance of D-Day, increasingly shrinking the picture until the reader might believe only Americans were on the beaches. Ambrose drew a sharp contrast between robotic Germans, "afraid to take the initiative," and American citizen soldiers who, "when freedom had to be fought for or abandoned, they fought. They were the men of D-Day, and to them we owe our freedom." Speaking of the GIs in northern France, he said, they "did more to help spread democracy around the world than any other generation in history" (Ambrose, *D-Day*, 26, 579; *Citizen Soldiers*, 472).

At times, Ambrose qualified his generalities, but others latched onto his phrases without nuance. Brokaw was one. Similarly, popular author Mark Bowden, in *Our Finest Day* (2002), introduced by Ambrose, made the inflated claim: "D-Day, June 6, 1944, was the climactic moment of the twentieth-century." The Americans (alone) won because "they were the soldiers of democracy. They were not as good as the German soldiers in taking orders, but they knew how to take responsibility and act on their own" (Bowden, 1). The actuality was often the reverse (see chapter 4), with the Wehrmacht encouraging flexibility, the Allies pursuing rigid orthodoxy.

Good War authors and their public seemed increasingly unaware or uninterested that six Allied forces fought in Normandy (U.S., U.K., Canadian, Free French, Polish in exile, French resistance). And the narrow focus on D-Day distorted the broader picture of the war. What of the other Western Allied forces that fought in Italy, the Pacific, on the oceans, and in the air? What of the Soviets and Chinese? The war had moments equal in importance to D-Day: the Battle of Britain, the massive German defeat in Russia, the Japanese quagmire in China, and their inability to hold onto Pacific conquests. If there was a single climactic moment, one might argue it was dropping the atom bombs.

Ambrose's second overriding interest, which dovetailed with his D-Day focus, centered on the American platoon. He almost made a fetish of small-unit male bonding. He took as a mantra the famous words spoken by Shakespeare's Henry V on the eve of Agincourt (1415):

> From this day to the ending of the World,
> . . . we in it shall be remembered
> . . . we band of brothers.

Ambrose's squad shares a transcendent camaraderie: "The social bond within the Army was like an onion. At the core was the squad, where bonding could be almost mystical" (Ambrose, *Citizen*, 332). Army buddies achieve a closeness unattainable elsewhere: "Comrades are closer than friends, closer than brothers. Their relationship is different from that of lovers. Their trust in, and knowledge of, each other is total" (Ambrose, *Band*, 210). In fact, the buddy system does provide important cement in a military unit, yet its potency can be exaggerated. Earlier authors, who had witnessed the war, projected more complexity. For example, John Hersey, in *The War Lover* (1959, filmed 1962), depicted a psychopathic bomber pilot who bullied the crewmen, his closest comrades, and finally destroyed them.

Ambrose was the historical consultant for Steven Spielberg's 1998 box office hit, *Saving Private Ryan*. The opening scenes of American soldiers storming the D-Day beaches are among the more realistic battle scenes in cinema history. But then the movie falls into the action-adventure mode, alongside *Raiders of the Lost Ark*. The implausible plot takes a unit of salt-of-the-earth GIs, in typical platoon mold, behind enemy lines in search of Private Ryan, hoping to send him home to his mother (who has lost three other sons). The fatherly leader of this squad is Captain John H. Miller (Tom Hanks) of Addley, Pennsylvania, a teacher, assistant coach, and representative plain American. Despite the absurdity of the mission, the platoon swallows it. Sergeant Horvath thinks it will even make sense of the war's carnage and earn them the right to go home. Actually, it earns them graves in France. Only Ryan gets out alive.

Adding to the fantasy, even though the Allies enjoyed total air and armor superiority in Normandy, the squad is bereft of air cover and only the Germans have tanks, so that the heroic sacrifice of the band of brothers magnifies into an Alamo moment. Illustrating the grip of myth, leading film critic Roger Ebert gave the film four stars and Leonard Maltin thought it a complex examination of men at war. Only Oliver Stone, a filmmaker and Vietnam War veteran, criticized Spielberg for promoting worship of the Good War at the expense of realism.

As Captain Miller lies dying, he says to Ryan, "Earn this." He does. Returning as an old man to Miller's grave, he says that he did not invent anything, cure any diseases, but worked a farm, raised a family and "tried to live my life as best I could. I hope that's enough." He is the ordinary hero of the Greatest Generation, stolidly bringing America back to normality. Meanwhile, also in 1998, President Bill Clinton, of whom much had been hoped, a second JFK perhaps, had committed sexual indiscretions that led to his impeachment. Inevitably, "Saving Clinton's Privates" became the year's leading joke, at the expense of a president from a seemingly lesser generation. Henry Hyde, senior house manager in the impeachment proceedings, declared a conviction necessary to keep faith with those who fell on D-Day. This was a bit of a stretch as FDR, Ike, and numerous Private Ryans had engaged in their own infidelities. But, in the mood of adulation of the Greatest Generation, nobody noticed the incongruity.

The next presidential election, between Al Gore and George W. Bush, too tight to call, led the Supreme Court to summarily award the contest to Bush. Although the son of a World War II combat veteran, the new president, like Clinton, had missed Vietnam, joining the National Guard, which was not deployed overseas. A year's gap in Bush's service record was never explained. But, after the 9/11 attacks, the media transformed Bush into a war hero, leading a new Greatest Generation. His speech at Ground Zero was dubbed Churchillian. Robert Kogan, in the *Washington Post*, called 9/11 a second Pearl Harbor, and Dan Rather of CBS declared a new world war. Tom Brokaw, in *TV Guide* (December 22), envisaged "a call to greatness" akin to 1941. Looking at images of youthful fire fighters battling the blaze, he declared America to be in the firm hands of a new Greatest Generation. So the best war would be relived after all, albeit under tragic circumstances.

But this scenario was not borne out. In the years since 9/11, triumphalist works have been eclipsed by more comprehensive, balanced histories. Clint Eastwood's 2006 movies, *Flags of Our Fathers* and *Letters from Iwo Jima*, represented more even-handed, balanced film depictions. Recent Good War references seem shrill, threadbare political posturing. When, on September 25, 2013, Ted Cruz spoke on the Senate floor for twenty-one hours, trying to block passage of a budget bill, Republican colleagues criticized him. Stung, the senator likened his opponents to appeasers of Hitler, but the parallel met derision. During the 2013 government shutdown, Rep. Randy Neugebauer publicly berated a female park ranger for not opening the World War II monument to veterans, even though he had voted to close this government property. Attacked as a hypocrite, Neugebauer apologized to the ranger. In a final example, Secretary of State John Kerry, in August 2013, challenged by a congressional committee to explain why military action was needed to rid Syria of weapons of mass destruction (WMD), replied it was to keep faith with those buried above Omaha Beach. Hyperbole perhaps, given Kerry had to know the atom bombs were WMD and that we used chemical weapons in both world wars, Korea, and Vietnam, where he served.

Quentin Tarantino's *Inglourious Basterds* (2009) marked the nadir of the myth-making. We follow the exploits of a band of Jewish-American soldiers bent on assassinating key Nazis. Their leader, Lieutenant Aldo Raine, demands each man bring back one hundred enemy scalps. He also carves a swastika in the forehead of an SD colonel. In a final tribute to the power of film fantasy, Hitler and Goebbels die in a movie-house gun battle. Anne Thompson said, in *Variety*, that it was fun to watch. Roger Ebert, gallantly shoring up the myth, dubbed it a big, bold, and audacious war movie. Serious writers disagreed. Daniel Mendelsohn said the movie turned Jews into Nazis. And Liel Liebowitz accused Tarantino of negating moral accountability in war, suggesting violence solves everything. Why this tarnished ending to the myth? The truth was it had always oversimplified history, misdirecting our thinking. But only in the twenty-first century did this misdirection become fully apparent.

Myths are not merely enjoyable stories; they help mold our policies and actions in the real world. To begin with, the relative ease of U.S. victory in World War II led to the conclusion that military solutions to foreign policy issues are usually best; diplomacy seemed outmoded. Because the United States was the only belligerent unscathed by attack, Americans understated war's destructive character. U.S. poet laureate Charles Simic, who as a child endured the war in Europe, notes that "of all the winners and losers in 1945, the United States is the only country in all the years since that has not experienced lasting peace, but has grown more and more enamored of military solutions to world problems." (Simic, 21–23). Much earlier, war veteran Admiral Gene Laroque said the same: "World War Two has warped our view of how we look at things today. We see things in terms of that war, which in a sense was a good war. But the twisted memory of it encourages the men of my generation to be willing, almost eager, to use military force anywhere in the world" (Terkel, 189).

In 1945, a hot war evolved into the Cold War, provoking a costly arms race. Andrew Bacevich, a Cold War army officer, said he grew up with the World War II myth of total U.S. virtue versus pure evil that transferred easily from Nazis to Soviets. He swallowed the belief that a dominant U.S. military presence was needed around the world to guarantee peace. But when the Berlin War fell, he saw the decrepit state of Soviet armor and wondered if the huge U.S. military outlay had been wise or necessary. What had it done to American domestic development? He remembered President Eisenhower warning against the growing love of war, noting the cost of one bomber equaled thirty modern schools or two new hospitals. Bacevich points out that the U.S. military budget exceeds the rest of the world's put together. An analysis of Obama's discretionary budget request to Congress, February 2013, lists spending on the military and veterans at 62 percent (with education at 6%, transportation 2%, and energy and the environment 1%).

Strongly supporting the doctrine of force as first option is the "Munich analogy," begun in the war by journalists and politicians like Winston Churchill, frustrated by the peace efforts of the 1930s. The argument runs that Munich proved you can never bargain with dictators; "appeasement" only makes the inevitable war longer. This is a damaging simplification of a complex historical event, justifying any and every use of arms. American commentator Andy Rooney said Hitler's worst crime may have been to convince Americans all opponents are bullies to be met with force. Ike used the Munich analogy in April 1954 to explain to Churchill why he had to support the French in Indochina (Vietnam). Lyndon Johnson used it when justifying escalation of the Vietnam military commitment in 1965. National Security Advisor Brent Scowcroft used the analogy to bolster arguments for attacking Iraq in 1990, forestalling sanctions, a nonmilitary pressure option to get Iraq out of Kuwait that might have avoided bloodshed. The Munich analogy enjoyed broad popular support. Victor H. Laws wrote in *Newsweek* (November 19, 1990), "My generation learned the hard way—a bitter lesson: appeasement quickly leads to disaster because aggression feeds on appeasement."

President George W. Bush and Prime Minister Tony Blair both used the Munich analogy to help justify the 2003 invasion of Iraq before the United Nations weapons inspectors had time to decide if Hussein had WMD (he did not). Bush had determined on war because he and Vice President Dick Cheney believed the first Bush failed to deliver a 1945-style total victory. The administration predicted a quick, complete victory, misreading the situation partly because they applied false Good War analogies. For example, Secretary of Defense Donald Rumsfeld mistakenly equated 9/11 with Pearl Harbor (even though Iraq was not involved in 9/11). Actually, all the two events had in common was that both were avoidable surprise attacks reflecting intelligence failures. Beyond that their characters diverged, suggesting different responses.

Pearl Harbor and other Japanese offensives were carried out by conventional forces, closely followed by formal declarations of war. The aggressor was a clearly identifiable imperialist state. The appropriate response was full military mobilization with an aim of forcing total surrender. Conversely, 9/11 was perpetrated by a handful of al-Qaeda terrorists without national affiliation (the majority came from Saudi Arabia, a major U.S. ally). The best response, proposed by distinguished military historian Michael Howard, in *Harper's* in January 2002, urged an international police action carried out quietly with minimum force and maximum statecraft, like the global war on drugs. But the administration's reading of 9/11 as a second Pearl Harbor, along with a desire to use America's huge conventional military resources, mandated a full-scale assault on a nation-state. The target would be Afghanistan, where al-Qaeda leader Osama bin Laden was hiding. The ruling Taliban government ordered al-Qaeda to leave but would not extradite bin Laden without evidence of his responsibility for 9/11, something the United States refused to provide. Heading a coalition of NATO and Northern Alliance tribal war leaders, Bush struck in October 2001.

The invasion failed to net most of the Taliban and al-Qaeda, unconventional forces that moved easily into the mountainous border region of Pakistan, striking back from there. The United States had assumed there would be no insurgency, despite the previous experience of British imperial forces and Soviets in the 1980s, deemed irrelevant in the light of American exceptionalism. Afghanistan became a quagmire, evolving into America's longest war; combat troops will not be fully withdrawn before 2016 and even then thousands of military advisers will likely remain. Over 14,000 allied soldiers and countless Afghans have lost their lives, yet al-Qaeda had only been displaced, not destroyed. We have paid a fortune and have not achieved Bush's outright 1945-style victory.

While the Afghanistan insurgency continued, President Bush determined on a second conventional war. In his State of the Union address, January 2002, Bush identified an "Axis of Evil," borrowing a World War II term to describe the alliance of Germany, Italy, and Japan. The phrase resonated with the public. The evil nations were now Iran, Iraq, and North Korea. Of these, Iran had offered help to the United States in Afghanistan, while no evidence linked the other two nations to 9/11. Nevertheless, using faulty British intelligence, the United States and United Kingdom attacked Iraq in March 2003. Once again, a quick victory was expected, and seemed to have been achieved over Iraq's weaker conventional forces. On May 1, 2003, Bush landed from a fighter jet on the flight deck of the USS Abraham Lincoln, coincidentally just in from Pearl Harbor. Against a huge backdrop banner proclaiming "Mission Accomplished," the president declared total victory in Iraq. In fact, an insurgency would drag on beyond the withdrawal of U.S. forces in December 2011, leaving a devastated country with hundreds of thousands of Iraqis dead or displaced. In this effort, billions of U.S. tax dollars have been expended. Following the World War II model, an economic boom had been expected prior to invasion but instead the Great Recession followed hard on the War on Terror. The circumstances of the two wars were not alike. Iraq's fragile Shia government is close to Iran, destroying the regional balance of power and, at the time of writing, Iraq appears on the brink of a civil war that has provoked U.S. redeployment of air support.

How could the Bush II administration have been wrong? Partly, in looking for precedent, officials always leapfrogged the lessons of Vietnam (the bad war) about the potential quagmire involved in fighting an unconventional ground war in Asia, to land instead in 1944. As with Americans freeing France, Belgium, or the Philippines, we would be welcomed in 2003 as liberators. Cheney boasted, "The streets in Basra and Baghdad are sure to erupt in joy" (Nester, 65). His prediction contained two errors. First, the memory of 1944–45 was oversimplified. Due to our overwhelming use of force in World War II, many civilians in ruined cities became hostile to our soldiers. Similarly, Iraqi and Afghan citizens showed no gratitude for the ruin of their homes and infrastructure. Second, late in World War II, we were removing alien Axis forces; in 2001 and 2003, *we* were the occupiers. Further, in attacking Iraq without the support of important allies except the United Kingdom, the administration had been partly misled by Ambrose and Brokaw into believing Americans could win major wars virtually unaided. Myth said America alone had saved the world for democracy on D-Day. Rumsfeld contemptuously dismissed French and German concerns as Old Europe irrelevance.

Brokaw's prediction of a second Greatest Generation failed to reflect the new reality accurately. World War II was fought by a citizen army of millions, chosen through selective service and roughly reflecting a cross-section of the nation. Our forces today are volunteers who represent perhaps below 5 percent of the population. To augment these troops, succeeding administrations, fearing the political consequences of a draft, have hired highly paid mercenaries or contractors. By 2008, they maintained a one-to-one ratio with regular soldiers. Not subject to usual Pentagon control, contractors like Blackwater committed gratuitous acts of violence on the civilian population, making "winning the hearts and minds of the people" harder, harming a crucial facet of counterinsurgency strategy. Erik Prince, Blackwater's CEO, maintains he was inspired to form his corporation by American heroism on D-Day. But, by 2009, federal records suggest he had also made $1 billion from military contracts, while America's total bill for using mercenaries may be higher than $85 billion. This is a different way of waging war.

Given the huge costs of the War on Terror, tax hikes, particularly on the wealthy, might seem in order. Yet, as we went to war, we cut tax rates, particularly for top earners, in 2001 and 2003. Justifying his votes, Senator Lindsey Graham said incorrectly that no additional taxes had been imposed in World War II. In fact, taxes did rise and salaries were capped at $25,000. The employment of myth often relies on such selective memory. Another example is the official use of torture, euphemized as "enhanced interrogation techniques."

Allied soldiers resorted to torture in World War II, but on a far smaller scale than the Axis, nor was it formal policy. Americans tried Japanese officers for waterboarding and condemned its use in the Cold War by the East German Stasi and other Soviet police. Forced to overlook these inconvenient historical facts, White House legal counsel assured President Bush torture was legal.

Although we used waterboarding and other forms of torture, the State Department saw no incongruity in continuing to publish its annual list of human rights abuses by other countries. In late 2003, revelations leaked about serious detainee abuse by U.S. military and CIA operatives at Abu Ghraib prison, Iraq. In April 2004, CBS News aired pictures of naked prisoners being degraded, threatened with dogs, connected to electrical wires, and deprived of sleep. U.S. world prestige plummeted, losing America much of the sympathy garnered on 9/11. America's belief that its exceptional virtue, inherited from the Good War, justified such violations of the Geneva Conventions had backfired, causing enormous political damage. The ethics of *Inglourious Basterds* loomed just a step away.

For many Americans, the fighting overseas seems increasingly remote, as they have no part in it; the Super Bowl is more lavish than ever. The War on Terror appears so dissimilar in character to the Good War that comparisons have faded. Even the Congress seems to have discarded the Good War model, closing down the federal government in a time of war, an act that would have been deemed treasonous in 1941–45. Accepting less than total victory, President Obama has withdrawn from Iraq and drawn down the forces in Afghanistan. Whatever one's position on the morality of drone strikes, their use to eliminate terrorists approximates Michael Howard's template of a police action. And Obama, in June 2014, made a shrewd, oblique rebuttal to the Munich analogy, remarking that having the biggest hammer does not mean that every problem is a nail.

During its ascendancy, the Good War myth perpetrated a paradoxical, gratingly cheerful view of war. It suggested that only through (perpetual) military conflict can we achieve lasting peace. This celebratory view of war is at odds with the experience of most belligerents in World War II. To believe the war was an uplifting experience entailed massive avoidance and re-imagining. Compare Ambrose's and Brokaw's prose with this statement by a veteran whose tone of thought has received far less interest in the popular arena. Captain Laurence Critchell here describes his reaction in 1945 to the end of the nightmare slaughter:

> For this strange state of mind which fell upon us for a little while after the guns had been silenced was a vague sense of obscenity. It was the faint, lingering aftertaste of having achieved something monstrous. We had unleashed powers beyond our comprehension. Entire countries lay waste beneath our hands—and, in the doing of it, our hands were forever stained. It was of no avail to tell our-

selves we had done what we had to do, the only thing we could have done. It was enough to know we had done it. We had turned the evil of our enemies back upon them a hundredfold and, in so doing, something of our own integrity had been shattered, had been irrevocably lost (Critchell, 384).

Buoyancy about the nature of World War II has hurt our view of the Holocaust. For over a decade after the war, Hollywood could not deal with its reality, even though movie moguls had visited the death camps, because finding a redeeming message of human transcendence from the gas chambers and ovens was so difficult. There was no higher meaning to be gleaned from the systematic murder of millions because an authoritarian government found them undesirable. But Hollywood was forced to try. American Holocaust movies tend to a redemptive tone, finding some angle to make us feel good and proud. They might showcase the minority of gentiles who worked against the final solution (*Schindler's List*, 1993) or suggest individual resilience in the face of oblivion (*Jakob the Liar*, 1999). Although most Jews had neither the tools nor opportunities to fight back, we celebrate the relatively few who did (*Defiance*, 2008).

The story of Anne Frank has been reshaped to provide an unjustifiably inspirational message. Anne and her family hid in an Amsterdam attic from 1942 to 1944. Eventually betrayed to the Nazis, Anne and her sister Margo died in Bergen-Belsen in 1945. It was death without sense or purpose. Filmmakers and authors have pretended Anne kept a bright spirit and faith in humanity, believing people to be really good at heart, an uplifting lesson for posterity. There is no evidence for this. She died ravaged by typhus, filthy, emaciated, and alone, her corpse, according to one witness, laid out in the mud like a log.

Alvin Rosenfeld, a Jewish scholar, thinks that any serious mainstream American attempt to confront the Holocaust has been still-born. He states, "Americans are typically given stories of the Nazi Holocaust that turn upward at the end rather than plunge downward into the terrifying silences of a gruesome death" (Rosenfeld, 62). Lawrence Langer, another Holocaust scholar, adds that although "there is no final solace, no redeeming truth, no hope that so many millions may not have died in vain," American interpretations still strive for a positive spin. "Upbeat endings seem to be *de rigueur* for the American imagination, which traditionally buries its tragedies and lets them fester in the shadow of forgetfulness" (Langer, 159).

Loss and grief did not fit well into the celebratory story of World War II. Good War writers do not dwell on the heartache and sense of betrayal felt by relatives of those killed in war. In the twenty years since the first edition of *The Best War Ever* was published, I have received letters from American children of men who died in World War II, writing of their lasting loss and their resentment toward those who thoughtlessly say they should be proud to be the offspring of post-humous war heroes or, worse, who simply ignore their personal calamity. Some question the price they have paid in missing parents.

I have a personal perspective to offer. One of my uncles, Charles Corringham Adams, a British Royal Air force fighter pilot, was shot down in flames along with his navigator on a night mission in November 1944, both dying agonizingly in the night sky over Holland. This was possibly the worst death flyers could suffer, according to William R. Cubbins, who flew with the U.S. 15th Air Force. "To disappear suddenly in the faceless void of night is to lose one's very existence, to become as an incomplete sentence" (Cubbins, 189–90). I am grateful to my uncle; his sacrifice meant I grew up in freedom, able to pursue personal fulfillment. But at times I, too, wonder if we have met our obligation to those who paid the full price.

Let us bring into the conversation Roger Waters and the pop group, Pink Floyd. Waters's father died at Anzio in Italy, a campaign neglected in our popular obsession with D-Day. In the movie *Pink Floyd: The Wall* (1982), highly popular among American youth, Waters shared his great loss, juxtaposing his sacrifice with the societal ills he sees around us: a failed educational system, skinhead racist violence, rape, poverty, and the drug culture. Waters was haunted by the mindless ecstasy of rock fans who filled his audiences. In a chilling fantasy sequence, he compared an American gig to one of Hitler's Nuremberg rallies, deliberately copying Leni Riefenstahl's 1935 propaganda movie of the staged extravaganzas, *Triumph of the Will*. Waters believes we have abused the legacy of family loss. There is no simple answer to such a charge, but we may be able to put it in a helpful context.

If Good War writers have downplayed the dark shadows of loss, they have tended also to spend little time on the shining idealism of the Four Freedoms, enunciated by FDR and Churchill in 1941. Admittedly, most soldiers ignored them, believing they were propaganda, irrelevant to their war. Nevertheless, our neglect seems odd, as these principles form an admirable template for judging the health of a democratic society (again, they are freedom from want and fear, freedom of speech and religion). In my bleaker moments, I believe we do not make too much mention of these freedoms because our report card is rather spotty. Let us take just one aspiration we committed ourselves to in the Good War: freedom from want.

Almost 634,000 of our American fellow citizens are permanently homeless (the figure rises to 2–3 million if we count those who occasionally sleep on the streets), living in loneliness and terror in our gutters. About 60,000 of the homeless are war veterans, many of them victims of mental wounds. The federal government draws the poverty line at $23,850 for a family of four. By that measure, more than 46 million Americans live in dire need. In our nation, 2.8 million children are in households that live on $2 per day. Their bodies are malformed, prey to disease; they cannot concentrate on their classwork due to the gnawing pangs of hunger. On a snow day, when school is closed, they miss their one good meal. During World War II, the income gap narrowed, but today inequality of wealth in the United States and United Kingdom has never been greater. A family cannot live on the American minimum wage. Successive British governments stealthily chip away at the welfare state provided as a thank-you to the workers who bore the brunt of the Blitz and sent their sons to die in two bloody world wars. Is there any breach of faith here?

Embedded in some Good War writing is the mythic concept of the Happy Warrior. Works emphasizing the adventurous aspects and powerful male bonding of life in a combat squad ("we few, we happy few, we band of brothers") have influenced generations of young men, particularly white males, to idealize the infantry platoon at war. As with all myth, a kernel of truth exists in this vision of a satisfying, shared, intense experience. But the dogface's life was also tedious, draining, often cruel, even horrific. Infantry were the disposable proletarians of the army, denied elite status (e.g., the paratroops) by lack of height, lesser physical or intellectual abilities, or modest education. While only 6 percent of personnel, they took 53 percent of casualties. And, as infantry lieutenant Paul Fussell said, for all the talk of buddies, wounds and death happened to individuals, alone and isolated. Veteran Joe Lanciotti said it dawned after a while that you were cannon fodder, the bottom of the barrel. If he died, he figured they would eventually build a shopping mall or parking lot over his grave.

The buddy system, in fact, did not hold up well enough to prevent thousands from deserting. Charles Glass, an expert on desertion, concludes: "The Second World War was not as wonderful as its depiction in some films and adventure tales" (Glass, xx). Combat veterans were unable to stop the glamorization. Infantryman Ed Wood said, "I puzzle over the way the war's reality was glossed over by stories of heroism and stoicism under fire, avoiding what the war had really been like—its pain, suffering, betrayals, battle fatigue, deaths, woundings, and killings" (Wood, x–xi). Public denial of the horror negated the soldiers' suffering. Joseph Garland commented sadly that the reality they endured was not transmitted: "The naked truth of humanity's (yes *humanity's*–) capability for beastliness is rarely conveyed . . . from one generation to the next" and so the human urge for self-destruction "persists in remaining a hidden mine shaft in the human experience known as the 'passage to manhood' " (Garland, xv).

Idealizing the World War II platoon can in a sense attempt to fit contemporary needs, a form of wish-fulfillment. Susan Faludi has studied the plight of today's ordinary, white, middle-class males, particularly blue-collar workers. Many feel marooned in a culture that no longer belongs to them, a world where high-tech skills and college degrees trump manual ability, and minorities with white-collar training can get ahead. Corporate benefits for production-line guys have eroded, job stability has vanished, and competition for slots precludes real workplace camaraderie. Faludi believes that nostalgia for an earlier, better time for the average Joe helped feed the popularity of Ambrose's model platoon of buddies, especially in the movie format of *Saving Private Ryan*, or the 2001 television miniseries *Band of Brothers*, based on Ambrose's book of that name. Faludi suspects that young men's engagement with the band of brothers myth stems not so much from a desire to take part in war as to find a model support structure that will hold up in changing times. Unfortunately, a long-past war is not a particularly good model for confronting contemporary problems.

Motivations for voluntary enlistments vary, including economic, educational, and career incentives. No doubt, some volunteers fit Faludi's profile of the stranded white male, along with equally underempowered African Americans. Disillusionment following exposure to the reality of combat may account for some of the emotional trauma of vets who expected a more meaningful collective experience. *The Yellow Birds* is a 2012 Iraq War memoir by Kevin Powers. As with many World War II infantry, Powers found battle's actuality disheartening, random, and meaningless. He was nauseated by his colonel's posturing, giving speeches that were a "half-assed Patton imitation." His platoon sergeant was an unhealthy father figure, a psychopath who "excelled in death and brutality and domination." He energized but also terrified his men. When a thoroughly demoralized member of the platoon went AWOL, he was captured and tortured by insurgents. After recovering his badly mutilated body, the platoon threw the corpse in the Tigris River so it could not be returned home to shock his family. Most of the men were terrified by asymmetrical warfare, where the enemy could be anywhere, all the time. They "stayed awake on amphetamines and fear." Powers concludes: "I'd been trained to think war was the great unifier, that it brought people closer together than any other activity on earth. Bullshit" (Powers, 19–20, 87–88).

Some Vietnam-era grunts felt betrayed by the heroic images that they absorbed directly from World War II movies. Lieutenant William Calley, facing court-martial for his part in the 1968 My Lai massacre, said that as an ROTC cadet he envisioned becoming an Audie Murphy. Some volunteers were inspired by John Wayne in *Sands of Iwo Jima*, the supreme surrogate father figure for an adventurous adolescent. For instance, young Philip Caputo enjoyed a cozy suburban life in Chicago, being a shoe-in for an educational deferment. But, inspired by Sergeant Stryker, he enlisted. Increasingly disillusioned by a war with no front lines, falsified body counts, and casual killings, he ended in an impossible situation, unfairly charged with murdering civilians. Caputo insisted that the previous generation had failed to say honestly what an Asian war against an alien people would be like. While in jail, Calley received letters from Pacific War vets saying they had taken part in atrocities. One said he was ordered in 1944 fighting on the island of Ie Shima to seal a cave in which a mother and twelve children were hiding. Such revelations came too late to help the 60s soldiers realize what they might be getting into.

Oliver Stone, another Vietnam vet, took on *Sands* directly in his aptly named 1986 movie, *Platoon*. Here, a unit of hapless, bewildered grunts is led into a My Lai style massacre by Staff Sergeant Barnes, a combat-deranged murderer. He is challenged by Sergeant Elias, a decent soldier whom Barnes murders. Stone has bifurcated Stryker to show us what can happen to any ordinary human placed in the extraordinary conditions of combat; *Sands* had failed to do this. To make his indictment clear, Stone has Barnes, before going into action, use Stryker's signature line, "Lock and load." Of course, the majority of grunts did not go to Vietnam because they were dazzled by images of screen heroes. Most went because they got drafted or just felt it was the right thing to do. Still, it is fair to say that a percentage who came back emotionally damaged had gone away pursuing a khaki-colored dream of glory.

Stone had trouble finding a sponsor for his movie, and it was criticized violently, as are most attempts by combat veterans to talk about the unexpurgated reality. The public rejected the implication that Vietnam was merely a more muddled version of the Pacific. Vietnam veterans remained a bad generation; World War II soldiers were the Greatest Generation. In May 2001, the media got hold of a story that Senator Bob Kerrey, a decorated Navy Seal who had been badly wounded in Vietnam, had taken part in a bungled special operation during 1969. A friendly local village leader had been mistakenly assassinated. The media had a feeding frenzy. Kerrey handled the attacks on his character with restraint, explaining that such things happen in war. But he allowed himself the pertinent observation that had the incident happened in World War II, there would have been no such uproar.

World War II is a seminal event in world history and correctly takes a central place in our study of the twentieth century. But if the mythologizing of this great and important event is at an end, that is quite probably a good thing. We have looked at some of the deleterious consequences of mythologizing the past. Above all, I think we do a terrible disservice to young people when we tell them that a better generation than theirs, a generation they can never hope to equal in public achievement or virtue, lived once upon a time in a golden age of war long before they were born. They do not deserve to feel from the start that they can never make as great a contribution to the public good as those who went before. To distort the past is to rob it of its usefulness as a helpful guide for those who come after. For each generation, theirs should be the best time ever.

Afterword

One learning theory holds that students will retain no more than three to four minutes of ideas given to them during the entirety of a lecture course. Similarly, the audience will take away from a book only three to four major concepts presented by the author. In summation, I would like to utilize this hypothesis to put before the reader four of the fundamental convictions that undergird *The Best War Ever*.

First, World War II was a complex and difficult event, full of nuance both in its causation and courses. It cannot be reduced satisfactorily to a few pat values statements or homilies suitable for use in any situation. For example, Munich did not show that we must always meet international opposition with military force. Nor did we alone save the world for democracy on the Normandy beaches. To repeat these shibboleths merely prevents us from understanding the full history and meaning of the conflict.

Second, I argue clearly that this was a necessary war and that Allied victory in part showed the strength of democracy versus authoritarian, militaristic regimes. But this did not mean the war was necessarily a transcendent experience for all, or even a majority of those closely involved. And just because this war was unavoidable and generated significant positive consequences it does not follow that all future wars will be the same. We should not assume from the experience of World War II that armed conflict is necessarily and always beneficent individually or collectively.

Third, I have suggested that all societies create myths out of their pasts to provide templates that help guide policies and actions in the present. This is a natural and often healthy process. But I have also tried to show that when our myths distort by oversimplifying history and diverging radically from its complexity, we make ourselves vulnerable to serious errors of judgment based on faulty premises.

Finally, I reject the premise that emphasizing the positive aspects of war, especially regarding combat, is patriotic and, conversely, that showing the full costs of war is unpatriotic. To keep faith with those who sacrificed on our behalf, we have an obligation to preserve the complete reality of their world, warts and all, so we may fully understand what they struggled through and hence fully appreciate what they achieved.

Alexander, Larry. *In the Footsteps of the Band of Brothers: A Return to Easy Company's Battlefields with Sergeant Forrest Guth*. New York: NAL Caliber, 2010.

Ambrose, Stephen E. *Americans at War*. New York: Berkley Books, 1998.

———. *Band of Brothers: E Company, 506th Regiment, 101st Airborne from Normandy to Hitler's Eagle's Nest*. 1992; repr. New York: Pocket Books, 2001.

———. *Citizen Soldiers: The U.S. Army from the Normandy Beaches to the Bulge to the Surrender of Germany, June 7, 1944–May 7, 1945*. New York: Simon & Schuster, 1997.

———. *D-Day, June 6, 1944: The Climactic Battle of World War II*. New York: Simon & Schuster, 1994.

Anderson, Karen. *Wartime Women: Family Relations and the Status of Women during World War II*. Westport, CT: Greenwood, 1981.

Babcock, John. *Taught to Kill: An American Boy's War from the Ardennes to Berlin*. Washington, DC: Potomac Books, 2005.

Baker, Russell. *Growing Up*. New York: St. Martin's, 1982.

Belpusi, Peter. *A GI's View of World War II*. Salem, MO: Globe, 1997.

Bérubé, Allan. *Coming Out under Fire: The History of Gay Men and Women in World War Two*. New York: Free Press, 1990.

Bowden, Mark. *Our Finest Day: D-Day, June 6, 1944*. San Francisco: Chronicle Books, 2002.

Brokaw, Tom. *The Greatest Generation*. New York: Random House, 1998.

Brown, Harry. *A Walk in the Sun*. 1944; repr. New York: Carroll & Graf, 1985.

Casey, William. *The Secret War against Hitler*. New York: Berkley Books, 1988.

Colby, John. *War from the Ground Up: The Ninetieth Division in WWII*. Mount Pleasant, TX: Nortex, 1991.

Costello, John. *Virtue under Fire: How World War II Changed Our Social and Sexual Attitudes*. Boston: Little, Brown, 1985.

Creveld, Martin Van. *Fighting Power: German and U.S. Army Performance, 1939–1945*. Westport, CT: Greenwood, 1982.

Critchell, Lawrence. "The Distant Drum Is Still." In *Combat: The War with Germany*, edited by Don Congdon. New York: Dell, 1963.

Cubbins, William R. *The War of the Cottontails: A Bomber Pilot with the Fifteenth Air Force*. Chapel Hill, NC: Algonquin, 1989.

Decker, Dan. "Transcript of an Interview with Bob Calahan and Art Crosswait, Veterans of the Seventy-Eighth Artillery Battalion of the Second Armored Division, December 8, 1989." Special Collections and Archives, Steely Library, Northern Kentucky University.

Eckert, Edward K. *In War and Peace: An American Military History Anthology.* Belmont, CA: Wadsworth, 1990.

Ellis, John. *Brute Force: Allied Strategy and Tactics in the Second World War.* New York: Viking, 1990.

Engelmann, Bernt. *In Hitler's Germany: Daily Life in the Third Reich.* New York: Pantheon, 1986.

Farago, Ladislas. *Patton: Ordeal and Triumph.* New York: Dell, 1966.

Field, Edward. Letter to the Editor. *New York Times Book Review,* April 14, 1991.

Fox, Frank W. *Madison Avenue Goes to War: The Strange Military Career of American Advertising, 1941–45.* Provo, UT: Brigham Young University Press, 1975.

Fussell, Paul. *Thank God for the Atom Bomb and Other Essays.* New York: Summit, 1988.

Garland, Joseph E. *Unknown Soldiers: Reliving World War II in Europe.* Rockport, MA: Protean, 2009.

Gervasi, Frank. *The Violent Decade: A Foreign Correspondent in Europe, Asia, and the Middle East, 1935–1945.* New York: Norton, 1989.

Glass, Charles. E. *The Deserters: A Hidden History of World War II.* New York: Penguin, 2013.

Gluck, Sherna Berger. *Rosie the Riveter Revisited: Women, the War, and Social Change.* New York: New American Library, 1988.

Graham, Don. *No Name on the Bullet: A Biography of Audie Murphy.* New York: Viking, 1989.

Gray, J. Glenn. *The Warriors: Reflections on Men in Battle.* 1959; repr. Lincoln: University of Nebraska Press, 1970.

Heller, Joseph. *Catch-22.* New York: Knopf, 1961.

Hess, Gary R. *The United States at War, 1941–1945.* Wheeling, IL: Harlan Davidson, 1986.

Hilsman, Roger. *American Guerilla: My War behind Japanese Lines.* Washington, DC: Brassey's, 1990.

Hitler, Adolf. *Mein Kampf.* 1925; Eng. trans. Boston: Houghton Mifflin, 1943.

Holmes, Richard. *Acts of War: The Behavior of Men in Battle.* New York: Free Press, 1986.

Jackson, Charles. *The Fall of Valor.* New York: Rinehart, 1946.

Jones, James. *The Thin Red Line.* New York: Scribner's, 1962.

Keegan, John, and Richard Holmes. *Soldiers: A History of Men in Battle.* New York: Viking, 1986.

Klaw, Barbara. *Camp Follower: The Story of a Soldier's Wife.* New York: Random House, 1944.

Knightley, Philip. *The First Casualty: From the Crimea to Vietnam; The War Correspondent as Hero, Propagandist, and Myth Maker.* New York: Harcourt Brace Jovanovich, 1975.

Langer, Lawrence L. *Admitting the Holocaust: Collected Essays.* New York: Oxford University Press, 1995.

Lindbergh, Charles A. *The Wartime Journals of Charles A. Lindbergh.* New York: Harcourt Brace Jovanovich, 1970.

Litoff, Barrett Judy, David C. Smith, Barbara Woodall Taylor, and Charles E. Taylor. *Miss You: The World War II Letters of Barbara Woodall Taylor and Charles E. Taylor.* Athens: University of Georgia Press, 1990.

Maharidge, Dale. *Bringing Mulligan Home: The Other Side of the Good War.* New York: Public Affairs, 2013.

Mathews, Tom. *Our Fathers' War: Growing Up in the Shadow of the Greatest Generation.* New York: Broadway Books, 2005.

Murphy, Audie. *To Hell and Back*. 1949; repr. Blue Ridge Summit, PA: TAB Military Classics, 1988.

Nester, William. *Haunted Victory: The American Crusade to Destroy Saddam and Impose Democracy on Iraq*. Washington, DC: Potomac Books, 2012.

North, Oliver, and William Novak. *Under Fire: An American Story*. New York: Harper Collins, 1991.

Powers, Kevin. *The Yellow Birds*. New York: Little, Brown, 2012.

Riesman, David, et al. *The Lonely Crowd: A Study of Changing American Character*. 1950; repr. New Haven, CT: Yale University Press, 1961.

Rosenfeld, Alvin H. *The End of the Holocaust*. Bloomington: Indiana University Press, 2011.

Rupp, Leila J. *Mobilizing Women for War: German and American Propaganda, 1939–1945*. Princeton, NJ: Princeton University Press, 1978.

Schlesinger, Arthur M., Jr. *A Life in the Twentieth Century: Innocent Beginnings, 1917–1950*. Boston: Houghton Mifflin, 2000.

Sevareid, Eric. *Not So Wild a Dream*. 1946; repr. New York: Atheneum, 1975.

Shirer, William L. *Berlin Diary: The Journal of a Foreign Correspondent, 1931–1941*. New York: Knopf, 1941.

Simic, Charles. "Oh, What a Lovely War!" *New York Review of Books*, October 10, 2013.

Stanton, Doug. *In Harm's Way: The Sinking of the USS Indianapolis and the Extraordinary Story of Its Survivors*. New York: Henry Holt, 2001.

Steinbeck, John. *Once There Was a War*. 1958; repr. London: Mondain, 1990.

Terkel, Studs. *"The Good War": An Oral History of World War Two*. New York: Ballantine Books, 1985.

Theweleit, Klaus. *Women, Floods, Bodies, History, vol. 1: Male Fantasies*. Minneapolis: University of Minnesota Press, 1987.

Toland, John. *Adolf Hitler*. Vol. 1. Garden City, NY: Doubleday, 1976.

Tregaskis, Richard. *Guadalcanal Diary*. New York: Random House, 1943.

Tuchman, Barbara W. *The March of Folly: From Troy to Vietnam*. New York: Random House, 1984.

Tyler, Bruce. "The Black Double V Campaign for Racial Democracy during World War II." *Journal of Kentucky Studies* 8 (September 1991).

Ugland, Richard M. "The Adolescent Experience during World War II: Indianapolis as a Case Study." Ph.D. diss., Indiana University, Bloomington, 1977.

Weatherford, Doris. *American Women and World War II*. New York: Facts on File, 1990.

Wecter, Dixon. *When Johnny Comes Marching Home*. 1944; repr. Westport, CT: Greenwood, 1970.

Whyte, William H. *The Organization Man*. New York: Simon & Schuster, 1956.

Wilson, George. *If You Survive*. New York: Random House, 1987.

Winkler, Allan M. *Home Front U.S.A.: America during World War II*. Wheeling, IL: Harlan Davidson, 1986.

Wolfert, Ira. *American Guerrilla in the Philippines*. New York: Simon & Schuster, 1945.

Wood, Edward W., Jr. *Worshipping the Myths of World War II: Reflections on American Dedication to War*. Washington, DC: Potomac Books, 2006.

Wouk, Herman. *The Caine Mutiny*. 1952; repr. New York: Doubleday, 1979.